FIRST THINGS FIRST

More praise for *First Things First . . .*

"As a former CEO and board member of numerous for-profit and non-profit corporations, I recommend *First Things First* find a prominent place on the desk of every board member and executive director of every nonprofit, large and small. An instruction manual and operating guide all in one, the book defines the path to organizing thoughts, structures, relationships, and activities toward achieving visions and values. The book clearly shows how excellence and success begin by doing the right things in the right order."

*– **Peter M. Hekman, Jr,** Vice Admiral, US Navy (Retired); now President, Business Associates International*

"I wish the IRS gave a copy of this book with every new 501c3 letter they issue. Tom has written a badly needed comprehensive performance manual specifically targeted to the needs of nonprofit managers and directors. These are hard-won lessons from a dynamic leader who's been in the trenches.

*– **Debra England,** former Organization Specialist, McKinsey and Company*

"As someone who has been at the helm of a young and quickly growing nonprofit, I can attest to the importance of doing 'first things first.' Tom's book provides insightful guidance and will help turn good intentions into a great nonprofit."

*– **Jeanne Liston,** Executive Director, The Hunger Coalition*

"*First Things First* provides all the materials and know-how to build a gold standard nonprofit. Tom's compassion for those running nonprofits, along with his sound business sense, shines through in every insightful and in-formative chapter. This book is a homerun for anyone with a passion to serve others through the world of nonprofits."

*– **Captain Key Watkins,** USN (Retired), First Commanding Officer of the Navy and Coast Guard's Wounded Warrior Program; now serves on the Board of Directors of the Navy Safe Harbor Foundation*

"*First Things First* is an enjoyable experience packed full of stories that drive home a number of useful pointers and strategies. I strongly recommend it to every nonprofit, whether they are in the startup phase, or languishing from stalemate. The book is organized and easy to read, and its suggestions are clear and easy to implement. It will be a bible for our organization."

*– **Dorit Dijk,** Founder, Green Lifestyle Film Festival*

FIRST THINGS FIRST

*A Leadership Guide to Building a
Gold Standard Nonprofit*

TOM ISELIN

Limit of Liability/Disclaimer of Warranty: While the publisher and author have used their best efforts in preparing this book, they make no representations or warranties with respect to the accuracy or completeness of the contents of this book and specifically disclaim any implied warranties of merchantability of fitness of a particular purpose. The advice and strategies contained herein may not be suitable for your situation. You should consult with a professional where appropriate. Neither the publisher nor author shall be liable for any loss of income or profit or any other commercial damages, including but not limited to special, incidental, consequential, or other damages.

Readers should be aware that Internet websites offered as citations and/or sources for further information may have changed or disappeared between the time this book was written and when it is read. The author has embellished some sections in this book for creative purposes and names used in stories are fictitious. Published in the United States by Pelican Lake Press. Printed and bound in the United States by Color House Graphics, Inc. Cover design by Kari Young. Photograph on cover by Dev Khalsa.

Requests for information or books should be directed to:

Pelican Lake Press
Box 250
Ketchum, ID 83340

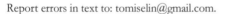

Or,

Tom Iselin
First Things First Consulting
www.TomIselin.com
tomiselin@gmail.com
858.888.2278

Report errors in text to: tomiselin@gmail.com.

Discount prices are available for bulk purchases.

Library of Congress Cataloging-in-Publication Data

Iselin, Thomas David, 1961-

    First Things First : A Leadership Guide to Building a Gold Standard Nonprofit

    Tom Iselin: 4th edition, 5th printing
          p.   cm.

    Includes resources and index.

        1. Nonprofit—management   2. Nonprofit—organizations
        3. Fundraising   4. Marketing
        5. Organizational Development

    ISBN: 978-0-9649139-5-0

Dedication

For Sara, who encourages me every day
to follow my passion of serving others,
and for Avery and Isabel
who bring me joy along the way.

~ ~ ~

All proceeds (100%) from the sale of this book
go to hunger relief organizations and organizations that provide
rehabilitation services to men and women of the armed forces
who have been severely wounded in Iraq and Afghanistan.

Thank you for supporting this mission.

Contents

The Author

Tom Iselin led a comfortable life as a stock options trader on the floor of the Chicago Mercantile Exchange. He successfully traded through "The Crash of 87," wrote a pioneering software program to manage traders' risk, and helped design software to run Continental Bank's first international stock options trading management system.

At age 30, Tom was on top of the world—so he thought. Then, one cold and stormy Chicago night, he had a life-changing, near-death experience. It was a wake-up call some people don't get the chance to answer. But Tom did get the chance, and the next morning, feeling God spared his life for a reason, he decided to exchange his trading jacket and selfish lifestyle for a meaningful, selfless life of helping others through sacrifice and service.

Tom soon directed his business experience and passion to the nonprofit sector and became a social entrepreneur. More than two decades later, he continues his mission of building, helping, and inspiring thousands of nonprofits of all shapes and sizes across the country.

Tom has founded or helped build six notable nonprofits that address some of the nation's most complex societal issues: Hunger and poverty (the Hunger Coalition), substance abuse (Natural High), the environment (Environmental News Network), people with disabilities (Sun Valley Adaptive Sports), traumatized, abused, and neglected children (Kids First Foundation), and one of the nation's largest and most innovative rehabilitation programs for wounded veterans (Higher Ground).

Having held all types of nonprofit positions, Tom knows firsthand the hardships of starting nonprofits, the frustrations of running boards, the pressures facing chief executives, the difficulty of securing long-term major funding, and the thrill of volunteering.

This diverse work experience combined with his extensive background in business, technology, and philanthropy gives Tom a unique perspective into the soul of starting, building, and managing thriving nonprofits.

Along the way, Tom made his share of blunders and stepped on toes. Years of hard knocks, lessons learned, and tireless work chiseled what is now insight and wisdom. He is passionate about sharing his knowledge and experience with nonprofit leaders to help them avoid the mistakes he made, so they can achieve success more efficiently and effectively, and with a lot fewer headaches.

His consulting services and vision to improve the landscape of social change through social innovation is well known across the country. Tom has written six books and speaks regularly at conferences and hosts workshops on the topics of organizational development, fundraising, culture, authentic passion, capacity building, strategic planning, and staff and board development.

When he's not working, you'll find Tom volunteering, playing tennis, snow skiing, mountain biking, fly fishing, or finding solace in his kitchen cooking and baking. He also loves to travel, hike, and spend time with friends and family. Tom lives in Sun Valley, Idaho.

Acknowledgments

I would like to thank everyone working and volunteering in the non-profit sector. Your tireless, self-sacrificing effort inspires me and it *is* making a difference. Keep up the noble work!

I owe a special thanks to the former staff and board at Sun Valley Adaptive Sports (now called Higher Ground – Sun Valley). Each of you used your gifts, skills, and influence to create a masterpiece, and the organization continues to soar thanks to your passion and hard work.

Sun Valley Adaptive Sports (aka: Higher Ground) is the focus of all the case studies in the book. I have chosen to use my experiences there to help others learn from the challenges SVAS faced while rebuilding itself from an organization on the verge of collapse into one of national prominence. I'm grateful to everyone at SVAS for making my time there the most thrilling nonprofit experience I've ever had.

Sincere thanks to Kim Mason, Celia Giacobbi, and Brenda Redfern, my star editors and proofreaders, and to all my friends and family who scoured the text looking for typos: Laurie Wood, Phyllis Huckabee, Dave and Nancy Iselin, Bobbie Iselin, Dean Singsime, Peter Giacobbi, Collyn Dixon, Eryn Michaud, Anne Gabriel, Dick Beaver, Pete Noack, Pamela Currie, Tony and Caroline Farwell, King and Cindy Lambert, Jim and Susan Morris, Sean Sell, Larry Brucia, Gail Kempton, Nanette Myers, Teri Iselin, Susan Werther, Anne Ramallo, and Olivia Wong. Everyone's keen eyes and useful feedback shaped a good book into a great one.

I would also like to thank Kari Young and Peter Fullerton for the cover design and Dev Khalsa for the photo on the back cover. Their work exceeded my expectations and I'm grateful for their willingness to donate their time and talents, knowing all proceeds from the sale of this book go to nonprofit organizations.

Most of all, I want to thank my sweetheart, Sara. I cherish her kindness and encouragement. She is a blessing beyond words and I treasure our relaxing afternoons of tennis, skiing, hiking, and backgammon that provide healthy and lighthearted relief to my busy workdays.

Introduction

Friends say you're crazy to start a nonprofit, let alone work in the industry. The hardship stories are well known: You work from sunrise to sunset. Family life will suffer. Getting paid means scraping by. It's thankless toil. Fundraising will consume you. Board members will disappoint you. It's a waste of your Stanford degree.

You have the talent to sit on the top rung in corporate America. You could make big bucks, travel first class, and live a cushy life with all the perks. This would be the good life for some, but not for you; you're driven by different motives.

You've chosen the nonprofit world because you burn with passion to fill the stomach of a hungry child, find a job for a homeless man, or save a teenager from abuse. You're compelled to make a difference—and you want to do it full-time. To you, it's not about Wall Street or State Street; it's about side streets and back alleys.

If your dream is to work or volunteer at a nonprofit that *truly* makes a difference, I applaud you. It's a noble aspiration and one of the most fulfilling experiences you'll ever have. My goal is to help you achieve your dream efficiently and effectively, and to get you on the track of success as quickly as possible.

Getting it right the first time

Starting a nonprofit is relatively easy. But building and sustaining a high quality, "standout" nonprofit is serious business. More than 1.0 million nonprofits compete for limited funding and resources in tough economic times. Donors, foundations, and volunteers have many choices, and they have high expectations of performance.

Succeeding today requires a team of thoughtful leaders making wise decisions. If you think you can scurry to build a board of directors made up of friends with little passion for your mission, you'll end up with a board that doesn't want to be accountable for anything, leaving you to do all the work and raise all the money.

If you run your nonprofit with a shoddy bookkeeping system, you'll soon find yourself in a black hole of accounting woes. If you recruit dozens of volunteers with no plan to engage them, you'll be left with dozens of discouraged volunteers looking to help other non-profits, and if you have no plan to nurture relationships with major donors, your funding will wither.

"Winging it" is the business model of many nonprofits. They race ahead with gobs of passion and ignore problems along the way. They take reactive, not proactive, approaches to growth and planning. The result is expensive setbacks, operational migraines, workload stress, and in some cases, dismal failure.

The greatest waste of resources nonprofits incur, and the greatest setback they face in their attempt to reach their potential, is spending time and money undoing costly mistakes such as replacing fruitless staff and disengaged board members, and adopting systems and structures they should have adopted much earlier in their lifecycle.

First Things First

First Things First is a guidebook for anyone passionate about running a high-performance nonprofit. It focuses on an essential set of governing principles, operational structures, and practical tactics staff and board members must adopt and apply to build and sustain an efficient, effective, and successful nonprofit—a gold standard nonprofit.

What makes *First Things First* different from other "organizational development" and "how to run a successful nonprofit" books is that the principles and tactics found in this book are often overlooked and understated, or leaders wait too long to adopt and apply them.

Failure to adopt and apply these key elements early on often leads to costly blunders and long-term consequences that stall or derail the dreams and momentum of fulfilling a worthy mission. Eventually, as blunders mount, leaders will feel like their nonprofit is sinking in a pit of quicksand, clawing for a survival rope that's one hand out of reach.

In *First Things First,* you'll learn why you should establish a culture of authentic passion before you nominate your first board member. You'll learn the power and value of hiring staff with superior writing and speaking skills. You'll see why spending money to build a brand is an investment, not an expense, and you'll discover how one-hour lunch meetings can help you raise thousands—even tens of thousands—in contributions from major donors.

The book provides dozens of practical insights, tactics, and tips, but most importantly, it teaches you how to *think* about the process of building and operating a gold standard nonprofit. You'll learn *how* you do what you do is more important than what you do, and just because you can do something doesn't mean you *should* do it.

Start building a gold standard nonprofit today

The nonprofit world is fierce. If you want to succeed and avoid being passed over or trampled, you need to stand out and stand strong. You need to be wise and you need to dodge disruptive, costly, and traumatizing blunders.

Three years from now, you don't want to look in the rearview mirror of history and say, "Gosh, we should have been more serious about building our social meida presence." "What a mistake it was to hire a chief executive who can't manage staff." "Wow, I can't believe the economy turned south and our funding dried up; we should have started a reserve fund years ago."

"Woulda, Coulda, Shoulda" is not the motto hanging over the doors of gold standard nonprofits. You've chosen to work or volunteer in the nonprofit world because you want to make a difference. To do this, you must adopt principles, practices, structures, and a mindset that will allow your nonprofit to thrive, not simply survive. This means, you need to do what's right, not what's convenient, and you need to do what's right, right from the start. First things first!

If you assemble a committed team and work hard and thoughtfully, and apply the principles, tactics, and truths in this book, you will achieve your dreams of building a vibrant and sustainable nonprofit that truly makes a difference—a big difference!

First Things First
Gold Standard Framework

You want to make a difference . . . Great!

You have noble intentions . . . Of course!

You have a worthy mission . . . Absolutely!

However, in your effort to make a difference, you face an assortment of difficult obstacles:

Obstacle 1: Recurring Challenges

1. Operating in a competitive environment
2. Lack of funding
3. Lack of people
4. Lack of time
5. Lack of expertise, influence, and general resources

Obstacle 2: Common Mistakes

1. Bringing on the wrong people
2. Focusing on the wrong things
3. Ignoring problems
4. Growing too quickly
5. Lacking essential operational structure and capacity

Obstacle 3: Common Resource Drains

1. Disengage, or under-engaged board members
2. Fruitless staff and volunteers
3. Undoing mistakes
4. Resistance to change
5. Waiting too long to adopt key systems and structures

This is the environment, and the struggle, many nonprofits face regardless of their age. They have noble intentions and a worthy mission, but they are constantly battling a variety of difficult obstacles that hinder them from efficiently and effectively fulfilling their mission.

Unstable framework

The reason why many nonprofits keep battling with these obstacles is that they operate upside down (imagine a teetering inverted pyramid). They think short-term, placing too much emphasis on "passion" and programming (the vertex of the pyramid). Therefore, as they get older and larger, they become unstable because they lack the key operational structures, capacity, and quality people they need to support themselves.

The result: Costly mistakes, organizational instability, lackluster performance, workload stress, stunted growth, and erosion of high quality staff, volunteers, and board members.

First Things First – gold standard framework

Gold standard nonprofits operate right-side up (imagine a pyramid with a broad, stable foundation). For growth, success, stability, and sustainability, gold standard nonprofits focus on what matters in the *long run:*

1. High quality staff, board, volunteers, and business partners
2. A unifying culture rooted in authentic passion
3. Steadfast governing principles
4. Healthy executive-board relations
5. A chief executive with exceptional leadership skills
6. A mindset of high-performance:
   - Efficiency, effectiveness, organization, and accountability
7. Sustainable funding and sufficient operational capacity
8. Programming with exceptional and measurable impact
9. A powerful brand supported by brilliant marketing
10. A valuable wisdom network
11. Doing what's right, not what's convenient or easy

The result: A comfortable business rhythm; clear direction, happy and engaged staff, board, and volunteers; abundant funding; exceptional programming; and adequate capacity for growth and sustainability.

The First Things First Framework is the framework you'll want to use to build your gold standard nonprofit. The topics in this book explain why these framework components (and others) are essential to your long-term success and how you can implement them to avoid many of the common obstacles that cripple nonprofits. Let's get started!

CHAPTER 1

Authentic Passion

Building a reactor core of commitment

oard members say they're passionate about fundraising. Volunteers say they're passionate about giving back. Local businesses say they're passionate about providing services. Staff say they're passionate about making a difference. It seems everyone is passionate about his or her pet nonprofit.

Well, that's the outside of the onion. Peel back a layer or two and you'll often find a veneer of passion that's big on talk and little on action—*lip service passion*. The truth is many board members loathe fundraising, volunteers make commitments they don't keep, business partners fail to make good on promises, and staff often feel a sense of entitlement.

As nonprofits age, passion tends to become more and more complacent and flaccid. What was once the compelling force propelling the work of a nonprofit becomes little more than a buzzword to excite donors, a hollow claim to motivate staff, and a worn-out tagline in annual reports. "We're passionate about helping kids!" Passion that once tasted like bubbly champagne now tastes like flat soda.

How does a nonprofit keep the fizz in its passion? It maintains a culture of *authentic passion*. Defined, authentic passion is how deeply a nonprofit believes its mission (ideology) and how genuinely and actively its mission permeates everything said and done, every minute of the day, by everybody connected with the nonprofit, in the relentless pursuit to fulfill and sustain its mission.

Authentic passion is the cultural spirit of a nonprofit. It's emotional, motivational, and contagious, and it suspends the conviction of those connected with a nonprofit. What distinguishes authentic passion from lip service passion is that it's constant, pervasive and visible—in everything. Lip service passion is talk. Authentic passion is genuine belief manifested in meaningful action.

In short, an authentically passionate culture is a "get it done!" culture.

16

Why is authentic passion important?

Nonprofits exist to bring about a change in individuals, society, and the environment. People who support nonprofits are agents of this change. Their passion, if authentic, stems from a set of core beliefs and values that drive them to actively and continually use their time, money, expertise, and influence to "get it done!" to make change.

The passion of all the people connected to a nonprofit make up a nonprofit's *collective passion*. The more authentic the collective passion of a nonprofit, the greater the likelihood it will flourish and triumphantly "get it done!" to fulfill its mission.

Without authentic passion taking root on an individual and collective level, a nonprofit will soon begin to wilt. Work becomes "work." Staff quit. Volunteers leave. Board members hide. Program quality deteriorates. Funding dwindles. Eventually, the mission erodes and the nonprofit begins to travel along a downward spiral of poor service and apathy from which it may never recover.

Authentic passion is a *First Things First* principle because the success and sustainability of *everything* a nonprofit does ultimately depends on it. Oh, you can get by for a year or two with one or two people carrying the authentic passion torch, but if authentic passion is not a holistic driving purpose shared by all, those carrying the torch will soon tire and the zeal and purpose behind their passion—and the passion of the nonprofit—will extinguish like a candle that's burned through its wick.

Case Study: Sun Valley Adaptive Sports

Throughout this book, I share stories, experiences, and observations from the five years I served as chief executive at Sun Valley Adaptive Sports (SVAS) in the small resort town of Sun Valley, Idaho.

I was hired specifically to rescue SVAS, and when I took the position in 2005, it was in crisis mode. The director, who also founded SVAS, had abruptly quit, leaving the organization in turmoil.

At the time, the stated purpose of SVAS was to enrich the lives of people with disabilities through sports and recreation. Although its purpose was noble, the organization was a dysfunctional mess, so there was not much "enriching" taking place.

At my first board meeting, I told the board it would take three to five years to rebuild the organization. I promised to build a gold standard nonprofit of national prominence with innovative programming, efficient and effective operations, and a fun and productive work environment that would rival the most noted nonprofits in our industry.

In less than four years, we produced stunning results. Programming grew tenfold. The number of donors grew from 50 to 800. The number of volunteers grew from 10 to 325. Staff grew from 3 to 20 and we had one of the best benefits packages in the community. Our brand attained national recognition and our budget grew from $150,000 to $2.5 million.

SVAS is an epic turnaround story. I hope you'll learn valuable lessons from my experiences there as you start or build your own gold standard nonprofit. I also hope you learn to avoid making the same expensive and time-consuming blunders the founding administration and board of directors made when they started SVAS.

Now, let's continue with the topic of authentic passion. During my first week of work at SVAS, I ran across six different mission statements and no one knew which version was the right one. There was no strategic plan, no fundraising plan, no operating procedures, no policies, no job descriptions, and no budget.

Oh, but there was passion. Most board members were quick to tell how passionate they were to help people with disabilities. "We're passionate about starting a Special Olympics program." "We're passionate about helping veterans who have been severely wounded in Iraq." "We're passionate about generating sustainable funding."

It seemed like board members were passionate about this and that, but personally had done little to nothing in six years to make it happen. Why? Because their passion was mainly lip service passion. Sure, they may have been *verbally* committed to the mission, but they were not willing to *take action* to fulfill it. And there is a huge difference between those who talk about a mission and those willing to do something to fulfill it!

SVAS was a ship stuck at sea; it had a broken rudder, no map, and its sails were luffing. Its board and staff talked about the destination it wanted to reach, but very few were willing to trim sails, swab decks, and navigate a practical course to take them there. SVAS seemed content to toss about in stormy swells, drifting aimlessly.

What SVAS needed was a plan and a set of tools, like the ones below and throughout this book, to get the passion out of their hearts and into their hands so they could transform lip service passion into authentic passion. They needed to stop talking and start doing.

Tactics and Tips
Authentic passion requires commitment and motivation

Does this sound like a script describing your nonprofit? Are you drifting? Are board members talking about the changes they would like to take place, but unwilling to do the work to make it happen? Do staff say they are going to get organized, but less important tasks seem to take priority? Do volunteers pledge to show up on time, but fail to show up altogether? Is lip service passion the mode of passion at your nonprofit?

If it is, you need to transform your culture into one where authentic passion is front and center in the hearts, minds, and hands of all those connected with your nonprofit. If you're a startup, you have an opportunity to establish a culture of authentic passion from the day you open for business and cultivate it so it doesn't become off-centered.

One of the core attributes of authentic passion is that it's an action. Action means doing, and doing requires commitment and motivation. What good is a noble mission if no one is committed and motivated to fulfilling it? What does it say about a nonprofit if the people behind it say they believe in the mission and then make excuses when it comes time to raise money, complete a job task, or attend a training session?

A noble mission with uncommitted, unmotivated people trying to fulfill it is like telling the world you're Santa Claus and promising to deliver gifts of joy to the Tiny Tims of the world, but then delivering stockings full of coal. Nonprofits operating in this manner dupe supporters, short-change clients, and rob society of social wealth. Eventually, word will spread and apathetic nonprofits like this will lose favor and fade way.

Commit to commitment
The first thing you can do to establish a culture of authentic passion is to commit to making a commitment to fulfill your mission. This means you need to commit to commitment.

Every person connected with your nonprofit must know and understand that the number one priority of your nonprofit is commitment. It's not the mission; it's commitment to *fulfill* the mission. Read that sentence again! Make the commitment to fulfill your mission your number one objective and primary motivation. Embroider this on your culture. Do this before writing the first line of your strategic plan, before asking another person to join your board, and before talking to another donor.

If you're an older nonprofit, you'll need to change the mindset of those connected with your organization. Start by holding a series of meetings and discussions with board members, staff, and volunteers to educate them about authentic passion and get them to adopt and apply this fundamental priority: commitment to *fulfill* the mission, first!

This shift may require an overhaul of staff and board culture and some of the philosophies and policies governing your nonprofit. Making large-scale change is difficult, so expect resistance. Be sensitive to people's feelings and opinions as you make a compelling case why it's important for everyone to make a commitment to fulfilling the mission his or her primary commitment. Emphasize that the success of everything the nonprofit does hinges on this commitment. First things first!

Authentic passion requires a clear sense of purpose

Your board, staff, volunteers, and donors may be committed and motivated, but if they are committed and motivated to separate purposes, your nonprofit will have no unifying purpose to propel everyone's work.

Another important attribute of authentic passion is having a clear sense of purpose. Successful nonprofits know where they want to go, what they want to do, why they want to do it, and how they're going to achieve it. They have a clear sense of purpose (intent) and it provides a backdrop for every important decision and action.

The three documents you'll want to develop to define a clear sense of purpose are a *mission statement, vision statement, and statement of purpose*. Embedded in these statements are the guiding principles and core values that create the unifying purpose to channel and propel the commitment (individual and collective) and motivation (passion) of your nonprofit.

In their own right, each statement is a declaration people can read to determine if their beliefs, interests, and motives match that of your nonprofit. They also create standards by which your nonprofit can measure its efficiency and effectiveness.

Once these core statements are in place, you should have a clear understanding of why you're in business, who you plan to serve, how you plan to conduct business, why you care about the work you're doing, and why people should support you.

Ah, but don't frame these statements and hang them on the wall just yet. You'll want to use the content and intention of these statements to write your articles of incorporation, bylaws, business plans, corporate policies, marketing materials, grant applications, job responsibilities, and various types of "case for support" documents.

Everything your nonprofit says and does should be connected to the intent and meaning of these statements, including how you manage staff, inspire volunteers, develop programs, and measure success. For example: "Do the outcomes of our programs align with the purpose of our mission?" "Are the fundraising tactics used in our major donor fundraising program aligned with the principles outlined in our case statement?" "Do volunteers know the core values driving our vision?"

There are dozens of books and online resources to help you develop a mission statement, vision statement, statement of purpose, and a case for support. I suggest you search out and read a handful of quality examples before you begin drafting these statements.

My objective is to show you the importance of these statements and to encourage you to make them foundational to all you do and say in your efforts to build a gold standard nonprofit.

Nonetheless, I know some of you are new to the nonprofit world, so I've provided a simple definition of a mission statement, vision statement, and a statement of purpose. This way, you'll have a basic understanding of what goes into these statements.

Mission statement
A mission statement should state what your nonprofit stands for, why it exists, and who it serves in a manner that inspires courage, commitment, and innovation. It should be results oriented, not activity oriented. It should be meaningful, measurable, and explain your intentions and priorities. Keep it to five sentences or less; three or less is better yet.

Vision statement

A vision statement should be a picture of your preferred future. It should be a glimmering, distant light that inspires your team to travel toward it. Design the content to be clear, uplifting, hopeful, and memorable. A vision should be aspiring and a big challenge to achieve, but it should also be obtainable and aligned with your values, culture, and strategic objectives. Keep it to a sentence or two.

Statement of purpose (basic "case for support" document)

This is a broad document often broken up into five or six sections. The first section should *briefly* list your core values and beliefs. The next few sections should highlight what your nonprofit does in terms of programming and services and the stated purpose for doing what it does, why it does it, how it does it, and why it's worthy of support. The final sections, if you choose to add them, should provide a brief history of your nonprofit, its legal structure, future plans, and funds you hope to raise. Keep it to three pages or less.

No matter what the age of your nonprofit, make it a priority to define a clear sense of purpose by writing or revising your mission statement, vision statement, and statement of purpose. Each should be precise, concise, and shared with everyone. More importantly, every staff, board member, and volunteer should be expected to know the content of each, if only in their own words.

Think about it. How can you expect people to be authentically passionate about your vision, and be authentically committed to fulfilling your mission, if they don't understand, believe, and value them? How can people effectively raise funds if they can't make a good case for support? How can you plan for the future, if you don't know where you're going? It's critical to lay a solid foundation before you begin to build.

Authentic passion centers on work and service

Okay, you've updated your mission, vision, and purpose statements. Good! Everyone says they understand the big picture and your intent, and everyone claims they're committed to commitment. Now what?

Well, it's all still lip service until commitment and motivation become manifested in work and service. The next step to developing authentic passion is to transform the *idea* of work and service into a *culture* of work and service. This may seem obvious, but we've all seen our share of disengaged board members, lazy staff, and irresponsible volunteers.

Define and assign the work
If you expect people to "work" (to "get it done!") at your nonprofit, and you should, they need to know what to do, why they should do it, and how to do it. This sounds elementary, but you would be surprised how many nonprofits fail to have a single defined job description or list of roles and responsibilities for its staff, board members, and volunteers. The result is apathy, confusion, and poor performance.

If you're serious about authentic passion, you need to determine what work needs to be done and then identify who is available to do the work or provide the service based on everyone's time, skills, expertise, and availability.

Below is a simplified matching matrix for a handful of general work and service categories. Build one for your nonprofit and replace the general categories with more detailed ones. This means you should replace "staff" with the names of each of your staff. For "programming," outline specific details about the type of work and service required to achieve your objectives and outcomes.

Needs	People	Resources
Operations	Staff	Skills/Expertise
Programming	Board	Time
Services	Volunteers	Influence
Planning	Contributors	Wealth
Fundraising	Partners	Services

This is a simple and useful exercise to get nonprofits *thinking* about how to accomplish the work they must do. It's the responsibility of the chief executive and managers to build a work and service matrix for each functional area of your nonprofit including operations, programming, fundraising, and volunteering. If your nonprofit is new, the founding board members can build the matrix.

After building the initial matrix, the chief executive and managers may want to expand the matrix to add "how" people should do their work, "why" their work is important, and "when" their work is due.

For board related needs, the chief executive and board chair (or board committee) can build a "work and service" matrix for board members, targeting board related responsibilities and tasks. Again, if you're a new nonprofit, the founding board members can perform this task.

This all seems rudimentary—almost obvious, doesn't it? But if it's so easy and fundamental, why do so many nonprofits have such nonchalant work and service cultures? Why do so many nonprofits have so many disengaged board members, aimless staff, and fruitless volunteers? It's because most nonprofits operate under a veneer of lip service passion, not authentic passion.

I suspect your hope for each person connected with your nonprofit is to feel that his or her commitment is making a difference to help your non-profit fulfill its mission and purpose.

Transforming this hope into reality will require your management and board to see to it that these commitments—*through work and service*—are defined and that people are held accountable and praised for fulfilling their commitments. When commitment manifests itself in action, when people roll up their sleeves and work, authentic passion flourishes.

Authentic passion needs reminding

How many board members can explain your vision and purpose? How many staff and volunteers can recite your mission and core values? The truth is, people forget. Most of us have trouble remembering anni-versaries and dentist appointments, let alone material from work.

If you want authentic passion to remain front and center in the minds of your staff, board, and volunteers, you need to remind them. There is no need to make a big production out of the process; simply set aside time on a regular basis to talk about your mission, vision, and statement of purpose.

For example, once a month ask one of your staff to recite your mission at a morning staff meeting. Write one of your core values at the top of the agenda you use for board meetings, and encourage your volunteer coordinator to share your vision at a training session.

What's most important is making an effort to remind people of your mission, vision, purpose, and culture on a regular basis, and that commit-ment to doing quality work is a primary objective and a core value of your nonprofit. Otherwise, the authentic passion you worked so hard to build will get dusty and stale.

You'll know authentic passion is alive and well when you hear board members say things such as, "Will this new program align with our vision?" Your board chair says, "What additional responsibilities can I take on to help with fundraising?" Or, your program director challenges a proposed staff change by asking, "Will another coordinator really help fulfill our mission more effectively?" When you start hearing statements like this, smile; you're on the authentic passion track.

Authentic passion is contagious

It will take a little training and a lot of reminding, but as authentic passion takes hold in the hearts and minds of staff, board members, and volunteers, their passion becomes contagious. They will want to share the deep sense of passion and commitment that validates their belief in your mission and the reasons they are involved. As they do, it will inspire others to get involved. Soon their authentic passion will blossom and they'll want to share their experiences, which will inspire even more people to get involved—and so the authentic passion cycle goes.

You can stoke the flame of authentic passion in your community by publicly sharing accomplishments, testimonials, and personal success stories about people connected with your nonprofit. Add these things to your collateral material, website, blog, and social media sites. You can also share them at staff and board meetings, volunteer appreciation parties, or during television and radio interviews. Give people connected with your nonprofit channels to spread their authentic passion.

Takeaways

Some of the original SVAS board members had tremendous excitement for the mission. The problem was they made lots of noise about the mission they claimed to care so much about, but did little to fulfill it. Like a faucet, it seemed they would turn on their passion only when it was time to talk with donors, secure a partnership, or bring on new board members. But it was all talk. It was lip service passion.

It took *two years* and a tremendous amount of resources to replace the SVAS board and transform a culture of lip service passion into one of authentic passion.

Can you imagine how much time, energy, and money SVAS would have had available for programming, fundraising, and operations had it not had to redirect these resources to transform its passion?

Luckily for SVAS, things changed and we survived. Most nonprofits exhibiting signs of widespread lip service passion do not change; they flail and flounder to the point where funding dries up, people leave, and the mission wilts like a flower that's been starved of water.

If you want to be a gold standard nonprofit, authentic passion must be one of your structural and philosophical cornerstones, and it must be the first stone, and the most stable stone, you put in place. As I said, the success and sustainability of everything a nonprofit does ultimately depends on it.

If you're a startup nonprofit, it's easier to establish a culture of authentic passion early on. You can include it in your bylaws, outline it in your statement of purpose, and hire staff and nominate board members with track records of authentic passion.

If you're an established nonprofit, you have your work cut out for you. You'll need to change your core documents, inspire staff and board members to change their ways (a huge challenge), and change the style in which you manage people and run operations. It will be like remodeling a home while you're living in it—expect the process to be messy and inconvenient, cost more than you budgeted, and take twice as long as planned.

The good news? Once you've remodeled your nonprofit and authentic passion becomes its driving purpose, profound things happen. Money flows in from unexpected sources. Volunteers offer limitless gifts and talents. Businesses shower you with donated services, and reporters call to write feature stories.

Most importantly, there becomes a steadfast commitment and a Ferris wheel of excitement by everyone connected with your nonprofit to "get it done!" and *work* with a pressing sense of pride and excellence to *fulfill* the mission and to share their experiences with infectious enthusiasm to all they know. Lip service passion becomes full-service, authentic passion and everyone walks the walk with honor, humility, and gratitude. It's nonprofit bliss.

CHAPTER 2

Culture

Developing a unifying force to inspire team spirit

D id you play on a high school sports team that won a conference or state championship? Perhaps you played on a winning basketball, football, soccer, tennis, ski, track, cheerleading, or gymnastics team. If you weren't a jock, maybe you played on a winning club team such as chess, debate, or band. Or, maybe you participated in a dance company or theater group.

Whatever the activity, if you played on a winning team, you know the importance of team spirit and hard work. Everyone has a role, every role is important, and everyone trains hard—individually and collectively—to achieve common goals.

If you reflect on those glory days, you'll probably discover you were part of a team driven by authentic passion, inspired by a respected team captain, and led by a demanding but compassionate coach who provided valuable guidance, praise, and accountability.

Playing on a championship team is a once in a lifetime experience. You make friends, have fun, and the more you win the more inspired you become to work harder to win more. It makes you feel invincible, your soul bubbles with joy, and the memories last a lifetime.

Working for a nonprofit is similar to playing on a sports team. Each nonprofit sector is like a sports league. It has its own language, rules, and regulations. It has its own geographic region: local, county, state, national, and global. Whatever "league" your nonprofit plays in, each nonprofit in your league is made up of people who believe their good work—their participation—will make a difference.

Some sports teams win championships because they have a star player. Others win because they have a great coach. Many have a star player and a great coach and still can't win a championship. Consistent winning requires more than star players and great coaches; it requires teams to have a *culture* that inspires and enables winning. A little luck helps too.

The same is true in the nonprofit world. Some nonprofits have a charismatic founder, an influential board chair, an experienced program director, or someone with an uncanny ability to raise money. It's a blessing if you have a star player or two on your nonprofit team, and the more stars you have on your team the better. But unless there is a strong team culture unifying the players and coaches, it's doubtful your nonprofit will ever win a major championship.

So, what is culture? It's the outward expression of *how* and *why* a nonprofit operates. It consists of one or more of the following elements: moral and ethical nature, guiding beliefs and standards, repeated behaviors, cherished customs, unspoken understandings, shared interests and values, and distinguishing style, character, and habits.

In simpler terms, culture answers the fundamental questions, "What does it mean to be part of this board?" (board culture) "What does it mean to be part of this staff?" (staff culture) "What does it mean to be part of this organization?" (organizational culture) For example, if I popped into your board meetings, what would I see? Excellence or mediocrity? Collaboration or contentiousness? Organization or disorganization? A "get it done!" attitude, or a "get by" attitude?

Why is culture important?

Culture is a *First Things First* principle because the most innovative and successful nonprofits—gold standard nonprofits—have a unifying force (an ethos) yoking the hearts, minds, and actions of those connected with a nonprofit to fulfill a mission.

If there is no motivating purpose, no shared value system, and no directed action, a nonprofit will have a dysfunctional culture. It will be unsure who it is, what it stands for, or where it's going. Work might be taking place and the nonprofit may be serving a set of deserving beneficiaries, and it may even have moments of greatness, but eventually its tendons will snap under the weight of uncertainty and it will hobble with a throbbing limp.

However, when the culture of a nonprofit is well defined, unified, and promoted within, it establishes a foundation on which every operational and programming structure can be built. The result is a *prevailing* culture that works together as a team, shares a common purpose, perseveres in the face of adversity, has fun, makes a difference—and wins!

Establishing a culture is also a competitive advantage because so many nonprofits know little or nothing about the importance of culture and its benefits. To them, running a nonprofit is like playing pick-up basketball—they hope they score a couple of choice players, hit a few three-pointers, and break a good sweat. There is little emphasis on practice and performance, and as long as everyone is having a good time, it doesn't matter if the team looks confused and takes wild shots.

Money and resources for nonprofits are in short supply. But teams that are intentional, willing to work hard, play smart, and learn from their mistakes will find themselves handsomely rewarded for their passion and efforts with one winning season after another.

Case Study: Family style culture

When I started working at Sun Valley Adaptive Sports, there was no culture. Well, that's not entirely true. There was a culture, but it was the limp and hobbling type.

Structurally, there were no strategic plans, no policies, no job descriptions and, like I said, six mission statements. No one was accountable for anything. Staff was unhappy, donors were disappointed, and the organization was operating a "wing-it" style of management with most of its energy focused on the fallout of its founder who recently quit.

Staff and board members had *personal* beliefs and values about the mission of SVAS, but there were no *collective* beliefs and values. There was no moral compass for the organization, no shared motivation, and no authentic passion. The culture was aimless and dysfunctional because no one knew differently.

My first few days on the job required no work of anyone. Instead, I tried to provide safe, lighthearted environments where staff, volunteers, and board members could share their feelings and express their thoughts, whether personal or about SVAS.

In hopes of getting people to open up, I decided to get staff and volunteers out of the office and board members out of the boardroom. We had regular meetings at coffeehouses and restaurants. We went mountain bike riding and hiking, and we hosted potluck dinners.

The goal was to spend time together to get to know each other on a deeper, more personal level. We talked about quirky habits and hobbies. We talked about hometowns and family. We shared jokes, tragedies, and dreams. I was curious to learn why the staff had chosen to work at SVAS and I wanted to know what motivated board members to join.

Each night, I wrote my thoughts and observations in a journal. After a couple of weeks, I reviewed my notes looking for common threads relating to values, beliefs, interests, and motivations of the staff, volunteers, and board members that lined up with the mission, core values, and purpose of SVAS.

The threads with the most overlap included compassion, wellness, fun, family, sports, recreation, adventure, therapy, and healing. These may seem like obvious threads for an organization that used sports and recreation as a means of therapy for people with disabilities. However, I found it interesting that the value and belief people talked about most was the value and belief in "family."

After sharing my findings with everyone, we agreed SVAS was in the "family" business. We helped families of all shapes and sizes that had a family member or relative with a disability. Our staff and volunteers cared for our participants like family. Each of us had a strong belief in the institution of family and felt family values would make a strong foundation on which to build the culture of SVAS. And so we did.

We started building our family style culture by developing a work environment centered on safety and sharing, not fear and oppression. At staff meetings, we budgeted time for staff to share personal challenges, relationship issues, financial worries, upcoming surgeries, achievement stories, and parenting troubles. It didn't take long before staff started referring to itself as a family instead of a team.

Over the years, SVAS did a number of things to build its family style culture. The board combined board meetings with dinner to deepen personal relationships among its members. Staff made meals for coworkers when they were sick, took camping trips together, and volunteered as a team to help other nonprofits in the community. As we became more and more like a family, we started joking, "Now that we're family, let's make sure we don't become dysfunctional!"

Over time, we became protective of our culture. When hiring new staff or nominating board members, the number one topic of discussion about the candidate was, "How would this person fit into our family style culture?" It was more important than the person's experience, educational background, skill set, wealth, or influence.

SVAS had a lot of messes to sweep up from its early days of management upheaval and operational calamity. Our strong family style culture not only helped us get rid of the dust and grime, it provided the collective inspiration and driving motivation we used to achieve outrageous dreams and accomplish audacious goals.

I'm often asked how SVAS was able to grow into an organization of national prominence so quickly. My first response is always the same: "We built a unifying culture early on and remained true to it as we directed our passion to fulfill our purpose." If you desire to build a backbone of success and gold standard performance, you need to do the same as early in your lifecycle as possible. First things first!

Tactics and Tips
Define a culture early on
If you're a startup, one of the first priorities your founding members need to agree on is the importance of establishing a culture. Once that's in place, you can move forward to assess the current culture, define an appropriate culture, and then create a plan to adopt a prevailing culture.

All of this will take five times more time and effort than you expect, and you can count on differences of opinion and a few head-butts. The most painless way to go through the process is to do it as early in your lifecycle as possible, because the earlier you establish a culture the more easily you'll be able to define it, fold people into it, manage it, and build an organization around it.

If you've been in business awhile, the task will be more difficult. The biggest obstacle you'll face as an older nonprofit is inertia. People—and organizations—get set in their ways and in most instances are reluctant to make changes, especially cultural changes, even if it means improving the work environment, relationships, and quality of service.

To overcome this barrier, find a handful of respected staff and board members willing to champion the undertaking. By taking this route, you'll find others more willing to follow suit and you'll increase the chances of a smooth and drama-free adoption and transition process.

If the chief executive and board cannot agree whether to establish a culture, modify the current culture, or establish a process of adopting a culture, hire a consultant. Running a nonprofit is difficult enough, so there is no need to create undue tension. A good consultant can facilitate the process, untangle knots, and keep the atmosphere civil.

I've observed all types of organizational cultures and discovered strong cultures share many of the same cultural attributes or "facets," as I like to call them. Many of the principles and tactics discussed in this book are facets of a strong culture (e.g., authentic passion, accountability, organization, fulfilling roles and responsibilities, empowering staff, etc.).

I'm sure your team will define many of its own facets, but the ones listed here and throughout the book provide a number of suggestions you can use as you begin to define your culture. What's most important is to make it a top priority to define and adopt a culture as early in your life-cycle as possible.

Establish a safe culture
No matter what type of culture you establish, let me suggest adding "safety" as one of the primary facets. People want to work in an environment where they feel safe physically, intellectually, and creatively, and where they feel respected and valued. Unsafe cultures, where fear of physical and emotional harm is prevalent, will cause people to withdraw and disengage, resulting in workplace tension and poor performance.

A goal of every nonprofit should be to create a culture where people are encouraged to be themselves and to express their opinions, ideas, and personalities without fear of judgment, harassment, or persecution. A safe culture creates a foundation for a happy and productive workplace and boardroom.

This is one of the reasons why it's important to define a culture early on. If your culture becomes unsafe as a result of hiring and nominating a few people that turn out to be disrespectful and judgmental, you'll find it difficult to change your culture into a safe one because it's difficult to change a person's nature. Also, unless a person has done something illegal, it may be difficult to remove them. It's always easier to hire people than to let them go.

So, if you want your staff and board to share a common set of values that fit into a particular style of culture, say a safe one, you need to be very thorough about the types of values, standards, and beliefs someone holds *before* you hire them or ask them to join your board.

Why? Because the nonprofit world is fundamentally a human endeavor. You only have staff, volunteers, and board members to run your organization, right? Without people, you can't do anything—you can't raise money and you can't run your programs. This is why it's imperative to bring on and *retain* great people because the higher the quality, the better your chances of fulfilling your mission efficiently and effectively.

On the flip side, we've all felt the pain of bringing on the wrong people, haven't we? We've hired staff that turn out to be lazy and incompetent. We've brought on volunteers that turn out to be duds, and we've nominated board members that turn out to be apathetic. The result: drama, wasted time, and negativity. If you bring on too many people like this, your ability to fulfill your mission becomes grim.

It's also expensive. Even if you lighten up the deadweight of your nonprofit by asking a board or staff member to resign, you'll have to spend time and money to find and train replacements. Plus, every time you lose someone, high quality or not, you lose "corporate intelligence." When people leave, no matter what their role, they take all their knowledge and connections with them—and in some cases, this can be extremely expensive, painful, and time-consuming to replace.

This is why it's imperative that you bring on and retain high quality people. To do this, you need to create robust hiring and nominating "filters," and then work hard to keep the people you bring on through respected leadership, meaningful engagement, frequent gratitude, healthy relationships, professional development, and an occasional good laugh.

Give people a voice
Another important cultural facet you should consider is "voice." Staff, board members, and volunteers need to feel empowered to share ideas, help make decisions, and speak up about something they don't like.

If you hire a tyrant for a chief executive, a bulldozer for a board chair, or a know-it-all manager, expect a divisive and contentious culture. Strong, self-centered personalities tend to squelch the voices and feelings of others. This will infect your culture with resentment and negativity, and people will feel their thoughts and feelings don't matter. Eventually, people will shut down, repel each other, and lose enthusiasm for work and service.

Make it a priority to establish a culture of open communication. Hire and nominate selfless, compassionate leaders who care for the welfare of others and encourage people to share their thoughts and feelings. If you do this, you'll find people more likely to participate in your directives and fulfill your mission because they feel empowered and respected.

Get personal

If you're in the nonprofit world long enough, you learn successful nonprofits have cultures that value and encourage close personal relationships. The result is a team spirit atmosphere that is fun, friendly, and resilient. "Getting personal" is another facet for developing a strong culture because relationships play such an important role in the success of nonprofits, especially emerging nonprofits, where the number of staff and board members tends to be small.

When you have a staff of six sharing a 20x15 office, it's difficult to hide irritations, phobias, and character flaws. Sooner or later, everyone's true nature unveils itself. The last thing a small and busy nonprofit needs is a reason to dilute its limited resources to babysit ongoing personal drama or passive-aggressive behavior.

One of the tactics you can use to develop close, personal relationships is to get staff, board members, and key volunteers to do fun, social activities together. For example, instead of taking staff out to a restaurant for lunch, take them on a picnic. Host a board meeting at a board member's home and kick off the meeting with a wine tasting. Host a chili cook-off and include spouses and children. Take a field trip to the state fair, a sports game, or to a museum. Volunteer as a team to help another worthy cause in your area.

If you hold a leadership role at your nonprofit, challenge yourself to lie back and give up control during team building exercises or offsite activities. The purpose of your time with staff, board members, and volunteers is to have fun and deepen relationships. The last thing they need when you're all out for a night of bowling is to feel like they are still at "work" with you controlling the show. Talk less, laugh more, and go with the flow.

One of my favorite methods of deepening relationships with staff is asking personal questions in team settings such as a morning meeting, team lunch, or on top of a hill during a team mountain bike ride. Timing is key and I'm careful to ask questions in a manner that flows with the ongoing conversation and seems natural. The goal is to get people to share their thoughts and feelings, and the likelihood of this happening is much higher if they don't feel like a local reporter is conducting an interview.

Some of my favorite questions include: "What is your favorite hobby?" "What's one of your quirky habits?" "What is the most unusual pet you ever had?" "What is the funniest memory you have of high school?" We then go around the table and everyone shares a response, most of which bring about howls and laughs for all to enjoy.

As relationships between staff deepen, I start asking more personal questions and the staff begins to ask questions of their own. "If you were forced to parent a foster child, what's the biggest sacrifice you'd have to make?" "What's one thing you've wanted to accomplish in the last year, but have procrastinated doing?" "If you could relive one event from college, what would it be and how would you relive it?"

These sharing sessions often take unusual tangents and pop the lids off traumatic experiences staff have bottled up for years. The result is a low-key therapeutic exercise that breaks down personal barriers, builds team spirit, and deepens personal relationships. No one is ever forced to share something they feel uncomfortable sharing. There is always an option to "pass" and answer an alternate question.

Strong cultures require healthy personal relationships. Spending time doing fun activities and asking personal questions happen to be my favorite methods to accomplish this task. No matter what methods you use, I suggest setting aside time on a regular basis to allow your staff and board to deepen relationships and build friendships. The stronger personal bonds you create with the people most closely connected to your nonprofit, the stronger and more stable your culture will be.

Care for others
Similar to getting personal, I believe nonprofits should include the values of "kindness and caring" as facets of their culture. The vicissitudes of life are inevitable, but they can be disruptive. There are no shortages

of people who suffer with the flu, struggle to qualify for a home loan, battle with cancer, face the death of a loved one, or find themselves without a car because of a dead battery.

A kind and caring culture creates a neighborly environment of helping others in need. When a board member is sick, have board members prepare and deliver a few home-cooked meals. If one of your staff is trying to qualify for a home loan, ask your bookkeeper if she is willing to help review the paperwork. If an intern's car won't start because the battery is dead, perhaps a volunteer who lives nearby could drive to her home and jumpstart the car.

So the question is do you show as much care for your fellow board and staff members as you do for the people you serve? It may seem a bit old-fashioned, but a kind and caring culture creates an environment where people feel safe, loved, and appreciated. No, you don't have to create a *Leave it to Beaver* workplace environment, but you can create a workplace where people can take comfort in knowing that if something in their life were to turn sour, a team of caring people is close by thinking of ways to turn their lemons into lemonade.

Reward staff with time off
One of the most satisfying things I like to do to deepen a culture is to reward staff with time off. Staff at nonprofits typically work longer hours and make less money than if they worked for a for-profit equivalent. Offering two weeks paid vacation and a dozen national holidays is a good start, but there are other ways to grant time off.

At SVAS, I rewarded staff by offering flextime. The entire staff loved to exercise and enjoy the outdoors (a signature facet of our culture), so as long as we didn't have an event taking place or a meeting, staff could take an extra hour at lunch to hike, bike, run, or do whatever. They also had the option to work through lunch and leave early. If it was a "powder day," they could come in a couple hours late so they could enjoy a morning of skiing in fresh snow.

Granting unexpected days off is another way to show appreciation for staff. I randomly gave staff a paid day off if they had achieved a major milestone, or had sacrificed a weekend day to work a special event. I also awarded additional days off during the holidays to create long weekends, and offered additional paid time off when staff members faced difficult circumstances such as severe illness, trauma, or a family death.

During my fourth year at SVAS, full-time staff received an average of seven weeks off a year. They also received paid time off to attend continuing education conferences and training seminars. Staff earned their time off, but it was also a juicy perk. They were proud and thankful for our culture, and it became the culture of envy of many businesses and nonprofits in town.

Adding flextime and unexpected time off to your culture will keep burnout rates down, morale high, and validate the hard work of your committed team. It will also help build a culture where staff feels valued, their personal time is respected, and their hard work is appreciated.

Reinforce cultural messages

Once you establish a culture, you must nurture it by reminding people. Your staff should hold meetings to discuss the effect of your culture on operations, administration, fundraising, and programming. Board members should discuss the topic of organizational culture, board culture, and staff culture at its strategic planning sessions. Your volunteer coordinator should ensure volunteers understand your organizational culture and how it applies to their work.

I found staff and board members appreciated cultural reminders. Sometimes I would send an email to staff with one of our values written in it, along with a blurb about what it meant to a particular project we were working on. At other times, I would facilitate board culture discussions at board meetings to remind members to work with staff on a volunteer project or to host a social activity to deepen personal relationships.

You'll find the more you talk with staff, board members, and volunteers about the values, beliefs, and facets of culture your nonprofit espouses, the more likely they are to adopt and uphold them.

Perhaps the best cultural reminder is the manifestation of your culture in the lives and actions of your leaders. If a facet of your culture is "openness" and your supervisors are willing to share personal goals, work challenges, and professional aspirations, you can expect your staff to follow suit. If your board has a culture where board members are required to spearhead an initiative, they will be more likely to fulfill their obligations if they know the board chair is fulfilling his obligations by spearheading an initiative.

In the end, sustaining a culture and all its facets is not a top down or bottom-up thing; it's circular. It's your responsibility, and the responsibility of your leaders, to draw the circle early on and continue tracing it throughout the life of your nonprofit.

Takeaways

A strong, well-defined culture is one of the key cornerstones you must put in place if you want to be a gold standard nonprofit. Once it's in place and functioning well, your culture becomes a collective mindset and moral beacon for all that your nonprofit says and does, and it becomes a powerful and unifying force to propel you to your dreams.

As a result, challenges become successes. Goals become realities. Staff and board drama fade, and all the people connected to your nonprofit *feel* connected.

It's important to create a custom culture to fit the needs of your nonprofit. I believe nonprofit cultures should be personal; create workplace and boardroom environments that are safe, kind, caring, and transparent; respect people and give them a voice; express praise and gratitude; center on excellence and accountability; and be advanced by compassionate leaders willing to walk the walk and inspire others to do the same.

But that's my take. The culture you create can include any combination of values, interests, principles, styles, behaviors, and identities everyone in your organization believes in and is willing to adopt and promote.

The task of developing a culture is a challenging one. You'll find the undertaking less stressful and the success rate much higher if you establish a culture early on because it's much easier to create a culture when a nonprofit is small, than to change one when it's large.

If you're in the nonprofit world, you're in the people business—staff, board members, volunteers, clients, donors, and business partners. And people like to work, play, and do business with people they like, trust, and enjoy being around, right? This is why it's so important to be patient and work hard to bring on and retain the highest quality people possible.

Once they're on board, you'll want to make sure you fold them into a strong culture because it's the unifying force and driving spirit your team of high quality people will need to win a championship!

CHAPTER 3

Organization

Creating order through efficiency and effectiveness

I f a major donor walked through the doors of your office, what impression would your office make? Are boxes scattered on the floor? Is garbage overflowing in trash cans? Is the carpet stained? Does it smell like Kung Pao chicken?

The appearance of your office will make an impression on how someone views your staff and your nonprofit, and if it looks and smells like a dorm room, the impression will not be favorable.

Okay, you say your office looks great, but what about your programs and operations, are they as neat and tidy as your office? Do you have systems in place to cover the workload of key staff if someone falls ill? Do you have a set of operating procedures to govern how programs should run? Are you confident your bookkeeping system can withstand an audit? Does your board have a system in place to review policies?

It's important for nonprofits to make good visual impressions. It's even more important they develop systems of organization to efficiently and effectively manage all areas of operations, programming, fundraising, and yes, governance. Otherwise, systems of disorganization will take root, and the more ingrained these systems become, the more difficult they are to uproot.

Why is organization important?

Organization is a *First Things First* principle because systems and structures of organization are fundamental to running, building, and expanding a high-performance, gold standard nonprofit. If you don't have these aspirations, then the dorm room model will suffice.

With a staff of two or three, a nonprofit can get by with little structure; everyone knows where everything is and how everything works. But what happens when the same nonprofit sprouts in three years and finds itself with five programs, 15 staff, 12 board members, 200 volunteers, and 500 donors?

Will it still be tracking donors in a spreadsheet? What will it do to ensure each volunteer receives appropriate training? How will programs maintain a consistent and effective structure? Can the board handle fundraising if the chief executive takes three months off for maternity leave?

If basic systems of organization are not in place, a nonprofit will waste inordinate amounts of resources trying to execute the most routine programming and operational tasks, especially recurring tasks such as paying bills, running programs, and hosting fundraising events. Without systems of organization in place, even something as mundane as a board meeting can become ineffective and wasteful.

Establishing systems of organization does not mean you have to create a stale work environment managed by hard-hearted perfectionists carrying sharpened pencils that dot every "i" and cross every "t."

Building and growing a nonprofit is a dynamic, lively process. Things change quickly and rarely does anything fit neatly into boxes. Staff and board members should assume change is going to be regular, unpredictable, and often chaotic. They need to remain open and flexible, and take steps to embrace change while maintaining order.

This is an important concept to understand and adopt because if your nonprofit has a mindset of organization and order sewn into the fabric of its culture, then efficiency, effectiveness, and performance become cornerstones of everything that's done. The result is fewer mistakes and headaches. This leads to increased productivity and use of resources—all without having to squelch freedom and creativity!

Being organized will also help you adapt to change much more easily because change in one area is typically less disruptive when all other areas of operations are running smoothly.

The principle of organization is essential to the short-term and long-term success of your nonprofit. Without it, you will stumble in the short run and may crumble in the long run.

Therefore, be wise and take the time to allocate the resources necessary to establish systems of organization and sets of structures, policies, and procedures to support these systems as early in your lifecycle as possible. First things first!

Case Study: Cleaning up the clutter

The first time I walked through the office door of Sun Valley Adaptive Sports, it felt like I was walking into a secondhand office supply store. Three of the four desks were broken. Two of the four computers didn't work, and there wasn't a single shelf or cabinet. The walls were tattered, the carpet smelled moldy, and the filing system consisted of a set of bankers boxes stacked on the floor.

The office wasn't the only thing in chaos; the entire nonprofit was in disarray. The founder had quit, leaving behind a disheveled nonprofit void of organizational structure. There were no procedures outlining how to run programs, no policies governing how to manage money, and no strategic plan to guide the organization.

I also inherited a tainted brand, negative cash flow, discouraged staff, frustrated donors, failing programs, and a host of other ailments that would send most executives running to greener pastures.

Much of the business was beyond repair, so instead of trying to patch its decaying foundation and leaky roof with blotches of mortar and sheets of tarpaper, I brought in a wrecking ball to level its rickety foundation so we could start fresh.

As hopeless as SVAS seemed, there were a few gold nuggets glimmering in the dust pile of the wreckage. The biggest consisted of two board members, three staff, and two star volunteers ready and willing to do whatever it took to rebuild SVAS into the organization they dreamed it could become.

A few weeks after my start date, with lattes in hand and determination in our hearts, we began the restructuring process.

We discussed authentic passion and how it should manifest itself in the lives of board members, staff, and volunteers. We defined a culture with all its facets. We voted to hire more staff and increase the size of the board. We wrote a new mission statement, vision statement, and statement of purpose, and we rewrote the bylaws and articles of incorporation.

The restructuring process was a massive undertaking and everyone agreed SVAS would now operate as an *organized,* professional nonprofit. A governance committee held weekly meetings to develop strategic plans and write policies, and the staff spent most of its time developing systems and structures for all areas of operations, programming, administration, and fundraising.

The ordeal was exhausting, but the result was worth the effort. In three months, we laid a foundation on which to build an organized and professional nonprofit grounded in best practices. It would take a few years to fine-tune the business model, but at least we had built a stable foundation that could now support skyscraper-sized dreams.

The doors of some of those skyscrapers opened sooner than any of us expected. In less than four years, SVAS was recognized as a national leader in two industries: the adaptive sports industry and the wounded veteran industry. We were producing documentaries, conducting efficacy research with universities, and establishing best practices standards for the industries we served. Our budget grew from $150,000 to $2.5 million and the number of staff grew from three to 20.

Many factors contributed to our success and amazing turnaround, but the most overlooked reason is the handful of hardworking, passionate people that worked day and night for months to develop a set of structures that allowed SVAS to *organize* itself. Only after SVAS organized itself were we able to leverage our resources and begin to grow and scale our programming and operations to meet the demands of our vision.

The lesson from this story is an important one: it's easier to build systems of organization early on than to build or rebuild them later on. Success is difficult enough. If you're a fast-growing nonprofit, you don't have the time or resources to unravel and rebuild disorganized systems once progress takes a foothold and momentum builds.

Save yourself a lot of time, money, and frustration by doing the right thing, right from the start: get organized! Or, spend the time to fix the cracks in your systems of organization before they get worse, so you can establish a stable foundation on which to grow.

I'm going to steer clear from sharing information about organizational theory; it's cumbersome and much of it is useless for smaller nonprofits. Instead, I'm going to share a handful of simple, practical, and inexpensive tactics you can adopt quickly to organize and manage tasks, people, events, and day-to-day operations.

Tactics and Tips
ToDo lists for everyone

I'm a big fan of ToDo lists. All SVAS staff members maintained a ToDo list and were required to send an updated version to their managers every Monday morning. Managers would send their lists to me and I would share my list with managers.

ToDo lists are easy to produce, portable, and provide staff and managers with visual snapshots of important work that must get done. You can use them to manage short-term tasks, long-term tasks, workload capacity, and phone calls.

I suggest keeping ToDo lists to a single page and separating tasks into a handful of major categories. Here are the ToDo list categories I maintained as chief executive at SVAS:

ToDo List Categories

1. Top priority
2. In the works
3. Long-term
4. Staff
5. Programming
6. Administration
7. Fundraising
8. Board
9. Phone Calls
10. Personal

Staff and managers maintained their own set of categories specific to their area of work. Programming staff added categories for daily activities and events. Interns added categories for errands and program support, and our volunteer coordinator added categories for volunteer training and event management.

The ToDos you'll want to track will probably be much different from the ones listed above. Develop ToDo lists based on the type of nonprofit you run and tasks you and your staff feel are important to track. If you're a board member, keeping a ToDo list is an effective method of tracking the tasks and work you're responsible to fulfill.

I required SVAS staff to bring their ToDo lists to most staff meetings. During our weekly Monday morning meetings, the most frequent question I asked of staff was, "What are the most important tasks on your ToDo list?" By openly sharing critical tasks, the entire staff had a better idea of the high priority tasks facing each department and how the staff, as a team, could help each other accomplish tasks and solve problems.

People go on vacation, get sick, and get summoned for jury duty. ToDo lists are lifesavers in these situations, since another staff member or a manager need only look at the absent person's ToDo list to understand and take over the important work at hand.

ToDo lists also help keep people from feeling overwhelmed. Life at most nonprofits is extremely busy and tasks pile up without end. Trying to remember dozens and dozens of tasks and details can create stress and tension. ToDo lists reduce the stress of having to remember endless amounts of changing information.

Smart phones, iPads, and laptops are useful communication devices, but I encourage you to have your staff print hardcopy versions of their ToDo lists and keep them on their desks in a visible location. Doing this provides a constant and noticeable reminder of the important tasks and responsibilities they need to attend.

My best friend's father once told me, "A good pencil is better than a good memory." These are wise words to remember. There is no simpler, more effective tool you and your staff (and board members) can use to manage and organize the tasks at hand than a written ToDo list.

The power of how
Order, efficiency, and effectiveness are central to the principle of organization. To achieve each, people need to know what to do, when to do it, how to do it, and why they should do it.

Great nonprofit leaders take the time to explain the "why" behind the work that must get done. Not-so-great leaders and managers, of which there are many, focus mainly on the "what" and "when."

Managing tasks in this fashion may allow a nonprofit to get a lot of tasks done on time, but it doesn't ensure that the tasks will be done in an organized manner, and it certainly won't be perceived as an empowering managing style by the staff and volunteers.

One of the things separating gold standard nonprofits from mediocre nonprofits is having a focus on quality, organization, and performance. One of the maxims the staff at SVAS heard a thousand times was: "It's not what you do, it's *how* you do what you do that determines the quality of your work!"

Anyone can write a thank-you letter to a donor or volunteer, but *how* a thank-you letter is written determines the impression it makes. For example, was the language clear, was the text personal and sincere, was the font style easy to read, was it formatted cleanly, and was it free of typos. Or, was the letter thrown together quickly and sloppily, looking more like a piece of junk mail than a note of gratitude.

You'll know when you've established a mindset of quality and organization when your staff starts saying things such as, "How can we improve the effectiveness of our children's program?" "How can we improve the efficiency of our annual fundraiser?" "How can we simplify our budget building process?" "How can we improve our volunteer training program?" "How can we improve the efficiency of our board meetings?"

The more your teams focus on the *how* behind the tasks they're responsible to deliver, the better quality work they will produce and the more organized, efficient, and effective your nonprofit will become.

Checklists for everything
Checklists are another simple and efficient way to manage tasks. They provide a set of step-by-step processes, a series of tasks, or a list of procedures required to run a program, manage an operation, or host an event. Think of checklists as scaled down versions of "standard operating procedures."

SVAS had checklists for everything. There was a checklist of procedures to follow to run our summer day camp, a checklist of what each therapist must record for each child attending camp, a checklist to remind staff how to start the bus, a checklist of what to do in case of an emergency, and a checklist to orientate new board members.

We also had checklists for annual events, employee reviews, strategic planning sessions, the process of managing donations, and the follow-up care plans we provided the wounded veterans that attended our therapeutic sports camps. If a system, process, or set of procedures had a series of important steps to follow in a specific order, we probably had a checklist for it.

If you're running a fast-growing nonprofit, you know things change quickly and the unexpected happens more often than not. Turnover among staff, board members, and volunteers can be high, and people unexpectedly get sick, take personal days, and resign.

If you have sets of detailed checklists, you'll feel more organized and less vulnerable to personnel turnover and absences because you'll have step-by-step outlines of how people perform your nonprofit's most important procedures and tasks. Let me also suggest that you store your checklists in electronic form in a safe and centralized location so staff can update and modify them with ease and regularity.

Once you begin using a system of checklists, you'll find they are simple tools of organization that shorten learning curves, increase productivity, reduce confusion, and improve the efficiency and effectiveness of all you do. Checklists are so useful you'll wonder how you ever got along without them.

Maintain a yearly calendar

Maintaining a yearly calendar is another simple, underused tool you can use to manage and organize your nonprofit. It provides everyone a snapshot into the future of your major upcoming tasks and events.

The more informed everyone is about what will be happening in the months ahead, the more efficiently and effectively you can manage time and allocate resources to accomplish the upcoming work and events. As with your checklists, you'll want to maintain an electronic version of your yearly calendar on a network, website, or some other place that's safe and easily accessible by staff, board members, and key volunteers.

A yearly calendar seems simple enough, but few nonprofits manage one. Winnow yourself from the chaff; add a yearly calendar to your tools of organization and encourage everyone to refer to it often.

Strategic planning

In simple terms, the purpose of strategic planning is to assess and discuss where a nonprofit has been, where it is, and where it should go. Strategic plans act as roadmaps to help nonprofits remain focused and organized in their efforts to fulfill their missions and achieve their dreams. On a practical level, the outcomes of a strategic planning session typically produce a set of corporate ToDo lists for boards and staff.

Strategic plans can vary in breadth and depth. They can cover a variety of business functions including operations, programming, fundraising, governance, board development, and staff compensation.

A good strategic planning session will cover topics centered on performance as it relates to fulfilling a mission and vision. Here are some questions to ask: "What's changed?" "Where can we improve?" "Have the needs of our clients changed?" "Are we on track to meet our fundraising objectives?" "What's working well?" "What's not?" "What new opportunities exist?" "What does success look like for us in two years?" "What direction should be heading . . . and why there?"

Going through the strategic planning process for the first time can be tedious and time-consuming. You could use a workbook or an experienced board member to guide you through the process, but for your first strategic planning session, I strongly suggest using an experienced strategic planning facilitator. If you ask around, you're sure to find a facilitator who will conduct the session at a cost you can afford.

A good facilitator can guide you through the planning process in a few days, along with some follow up, if everyone is prepared and eager to work. They will also make the process fun and insightful, and bring a neutral voice to the process. A neutral voice is essential, because it will help reduce any tension that may exist between board members, or more likely, between board members and the chief executive.

Make sure you involve key staff in the planning process because they know the needs of your clients, operations, and programming better than anyone.

At SVAS, staff held their own strategic planning session for operations and programming one month before the board held its corporate strategic planning session. The outcomes of the staff's planning session became primary reference documents for the board's planning process.

Too many nonprofits blow off strategic planning. They fail to see the benefit or feel it's a waste of time. They are content being lost and disorganized and twiddle their thumbs about direction and purpose.

Think about it. How can you achieve a dream if you have no plan to make it happen? How can you measure performance if you haven't decided what to measure? How can you flank threats if you haven't addressed them?

Make a smart decision about getting organized. Commit to developing a simple, focused strategic plan that assigns tasks and holds people accountable; it's your atlas for traveling the roads of success.

Create a budget

The purpose of a budget is to help forecast and manage income, expenses, and cash flow. Knowing how money flows in and out of your nonprofit is essential if you want to run an efficient, effective, and well-organized nonprofit.

Building a budget, like building a strategic plan, can be a confusing and time-consuming process. If you don't know how to build a budget, seek the advice of an experienced bookkeeper, accountant, or nonprofit executive to walk you through the process.

Even if you know how to create a budget, you should still have an experienced bookkeeper or accountant review it. They live in a world of finance and numbers and will probably notice things you overlooked.

Going through the budgeting process for the first time, or anytime for that matter, is usually an eye-opening exercise. Budgets expose financial weaknesses and challenge financial assumptions. You may discover medical benefits cost double what you thought. You may learn April through June are your weakest cash flow months, and you may notice your least attended program costs the most amount of money to operate.

When building a budget, fold key managers into the process. They can provide valuable insights about expenses specific to the programs and work they oversee.

At SVAS, I provided each manager with a skeleton budget for their area of responsibility based on figures from the previous year's budget. Managers worked with their staff and our bookkeeper to build their budgets. I then reviewed each budget with the managers and we made modifications as needed.

The next step was aggregating the program budgets with the budgets for administration and fundraising to create a single, comprehensive budget. This budget was then presented to our finance committee for review. After listening to their suggestions and making changes, I would present a final version of the budget to the full board for approval. This entire process was repeated each spring.

Forecast income and expenses
Probably the most common mistake nonprofits make when budgeting is overestimating income and underestimating expenses. This can spell disaster when actual figures fail to meet expectations. To reduce this risk, reduce the amount of income you forecast by 20 percent and increase the amount of expenses you forecast by 20 percent.

This simple adjustment will create a margin of error large enough to accommodate most fluctuations in income and expenses that will happen throughout the year.

It's important to remind your staff and board members to think of budgets in terms of targets and guidelines, not contracts etched in stone. This may be more difficult than you think, because there is always one board member who insists his nonprofit should "toe-the-line" with every expense. When he notices any deviation from the budget he snaps, "We're over budget, let's discuss it!"

Ironically, if the same nonprofit received an unexpected gift of $50,000, I doubt very much the same board member would say, "We're over budget on income, let's discuss it!" This double standard is absurd and any board member who squawks about petty budget deviations should spend more time raising money and less time complaining.

Of course, if you spot a major trend of increasing expenses, or one particular expense or disbursement that is exceptionally high in a given month, the chief executive should address the cause and share it with the board if necessary.

Create a reserve fund
This reminds me of an important point. You should set aside a percentage of your income every year and put it into a *reserve fund*. Reserve funds are important because many nonprofits face times of unexpected expenses and sudden downturns in donations.

Having funds in reserve provides financial security to assuage the impact of such surprises. Also, when the fund is large enough, you can direct a portion of the funds for capacity building, hiring staff, paying down debt, or starting an endowment.

Some nonprofits add a fixed sum of money to their reserve fund every year, say $25,000. They include this figure in their budgets as a line item and establish fundraising goals to raise this sum.

Others build reserve funds by putting aside a percentage of the income they raise in a year after paying all their expenses. For example, if you raised $500,000 last year and your expenses were $400,000, you may decide to set aside 20 percent of your excess income ($100,000) in reserve ($20,000).

Improve your chances of getting funded
One of the understated benefits of building a high quality budget is its ability to help nonprofits raise money. Foundations and many major donors will require you to submit a budget before funding you. If your budget is thorough, easy-to-understand, and professional looking it will greatly improve your chances of getting funded, since many nonprofits produce shoddy, difficult to read budgets.

Yes, building a budget can be an annual pain in the butt. However, if you build good ones, you'll find them to be one of the best tools you can use to organize, plan, manage, forecast, and raise money. Tough work has its rewards.

Use professionals to get your books in order
Great budgets depend on accurate figures. Accurate figures require good systems of bookkeeping and accounting. A good system of bookkeeping and accounting requires the services of *professional* bookkeepers and accountants. It's a simple chain, one you must connect if you want your finances to be organized and precise.

Many nonprofits make the mistake of adopting for-profit bookkeeping and accounting practices because they think these practices are the same for both for-profits and nonprofits. They are not. They are quite distinct. You need to realize this before you enter your first receipt. If you don't, you're in for an agonizing and expensive confrontation with regret.

Nonprofit accounting is set up to handle circumstances unique to running a nonprofit. For example, how would you account for a donated car? What if a donor wants to set up an annuity trust? What if a business partner decides to transfer shares of stock to your nonprofit? What type of reporting is required if your endowment offers scholarships? How do you account for time sensitive restricted donations?

Nonprofit accounting is set up to handle such things, and the faster you grow, the more complicated your bookkeeping and accounting will become. How do you plan to pay unemployment insurance? How do you plan to track payroll, vacation time, and medical insurance? Who's going to make deposits, pay bills, and call businesses that owe money? Who will complete your 990 tax reporting documents and file them with the IRS?

An experienced bookkeeper specializing in nonprofit bookkeeping will know how to handle such things. This is why it's important you hire an experienced bookkeeper with nonprofit experience. Let me say this again—with *nonprofit* experience. The same holds true for your accountant. Hiring a bookkeeper or accountant without nonprofit experience is like hiring a knee surgeon to perform eye surgery—you'll get a surgeon, but the outcome could be disastrous and may leave you blind.

Too often, nonprofits ask a volunteer to manage their books or hire a part-time bookkeeper with little or no nonprofit accounting background. It's a noble gesture for those willing to help, but trust me, as you begin to grow, ad hoc systems and inexperienced help will become recurring nightmares. You'll end up with massive headaches and enormous bills as you attempt to fix a bottomless pit of problems.

There are other reasons to have your books in order. Your board members are legally liable for the financial integrity of your nonprofit. If they are wise, they will expect impeccable books because they understand the legal consequences and public embarrassment that could come about as a result of misreporting or misrepresenting financial information.

Professional bookkeeping and accounting will also prove invaluable as you raise money. I touched on this earlier, but it's worth mentioning again. In the eyes of foundations and major donors, organized accounting systems and accurate financial statements will place you head-and-shoulders above most nonprofits because so many use ad hoc and disorganized systems of accounting and financial reporting.

Do yourself and your nonprofit a colossal favor and hire the best nonprofit bookkeeper and accountant you can afford as soon as possible. From day one, your books will be impeccable and your financial systems will be organized and efficient. When you look back five years from now, it will prove to be one of the smartest decisions you made.

Takeaways

I've never met a donor that toured through the offices of a nonprofit and said, "Wow, this place is a dump, staff seem confused, the board is disengaged, and you don't have a strategic plan or a budget . . . no problem, I would love to donate $10,000!"

If a handful of major donors walked into your office, how would they rate your ability to run an organized nonprofit based on their visual impression? On a scale of 1 to 10, how efficiently and effectively would they say you manage programs, run operations, engage board members, and achieve fundraising goals? How would they rate your ability to plan for the future or measure past performance? How would they rate the quality and organization of your bookkeeping and accounting practices?

When a nonprofit is young and small, it's easy to get by with little structure. It doesn't take much effort to manage one or two programs, a few staff, and a handful of volunteers. Each staff knows who's doing what and everyone can manage his or her work using his or her own systems of organization with little guidance. Laissez-faire works.

However, as a nonprofit grows, especially if it grows at a rate of 50 to 100 percent a year, operational structures of all types quickly become strained. In fact, one of the greatest stressors nonprofits face is changing or implementing a major operational structure in the middle of a growth surge.

For example, let's say the system you use to train five volunteers takes two hours per week per volunteer. What if you suddenly find yourself training 200 volunteers? Who's going to do the training? How will you do it?

With only a handful of bookkeeping transactions a month, you may be able to manage your books in a spreadsheet, but how will you manage your books when the number of transactions jumps to 2000 a month?

Adapting to changes such as these would be a lot more manageable if you could cease operations for three months while fine-tuning the tools and structures needed to handle increased capacity or to replace old systems with new ones.

Well, that's not going to happen. Participants rely on you to provide services, volunteers expect you to keep in touch, businesses count on you to pay bills, and staff rely on you to pay wages. You can't just stop operations every time you need to make a major structural change.

Many nonprofits encounter this growth-change predicament. They want to add new structures or replace old ones to be more efficient, effective, and organized, yet they must remain operational while making the changes. The impact can be daunting and can bring a nonprofit to its knees if it's not careful.

You must be acutely aware of how disruptive change can be to the rhythm of your nonprofit. You must also accept the fact that change is a way of life at nonprofits and prepare for change by establishing a culture and mindset of organization, supported by systems and structures of organization to help you manage change.

Simple tools such as ToDo lists, checklists, and yearly calendars will keep everyone informed about who is doing what and when. Widespread structural components such as strategic plans, budgets, and bookkeeping systems will provide guidance and insight to help you raise funds, manage operations, and leverage resources to scale programming and operations, as well as keep you on track to fulfill your mission.

Applying these tools alone will save you months—and in some cases years—of painful disruptions and setbacks. They will also help you raise money, grow faster, operate smoothly, and run your nonprofit in an organized and effective manner. Remember, it's not what you do, it's *how* you do what you do that makes a difference!

Super timesaving tip for board meetings: Use a consent agenda! Send me an email at tomiselin@gmail.com and I'll send you a free template.

CHAPTER 4

Writing

Transforming words into power and influence

When was the last time you received a handwritten letter? Not an invitation or thank-you card, I'm talking about a hand-written, personal letter written on paper. If you're like most Americans, it's probably been a while.

The art of writing letters, and writing in general, has fallen by the way-side. We live in a world of smart phones, emails, text messages, Skype, and LinkedIn. Handwriting feels foreign to most of us. When we do write, our sentences are chock-full of acronyms and errors, and our penmanship is atrocious. We dodge opportunities to write whenever we can, though we never cease to smile when we open our mailboxes and discover a handwritten letter addressed to us.

Writing is a skill learned early in life, and most of us disliked writing and grammar classes as much as we disliked eating vegetables. Our distaste for writing followed us into adulthood because we still suffer from the same writing inadequacies we had in childhood. We suffer writer's block. We struggle to organize thoughts. We spell poorly, and we know less grammar and sentence structure now than when we played tetherball. It's all very humbling.

Why is writing important?

Writing is a *First Things First* principle because good writing is a tool of tremendous power, influence, and leverage. A single compelling press release might land you a national television interview that leads to 100 new donors and $100,000 in funding. A motivating flyer could inspire dozens of people to volunteer for your new program, and a persuasive letter to a senator might inspire new legislation.

The nonprofit world swims in an ocean of written documents. There are annual reports, grant applications, website pages, blogs, appeal letters, policy documents, procedure manuals, thank-you notes, press releases, program reports, research papers, legal documents, advertising copy, board orientation documents, promotional material, and much more.

Each of these communication vehicles influences its readers in some way. Each will make positive or negative impressions on a reader about the nonprofit, the person who wrote the material, and the concept or ideas expressed in the material. The result could mean the difference between whether or not a nonprofit receives a major grant, acquires a new donor, or secures a key partnership.

Good writing often goes unnoticed, but poor writing doesn't. It can create lasting, negative impressions. Most people will forgive an occasional grammar or spelling error (you may even find a few in this book), but writing letter after letter and document after document littered with spelling errors, grammatical mistakes, and choppy sentence flow will dilute the credibility of a writer—and a nonprofit. Not good.

You may have only one chance to make a good impression, so you want to make each impression, especially a written impression, the best it can be. To do that, you need to value quality writing as much as you value quality programming, and you need to adopt a culture of quality writing as early in your lifecycle as possible to harness its power and influence. First things first!

Case Study: The lost art of writing

Sun Valley Adaptive Sports once excelled in shoddy writing. The founding administration put little time or effort into the written word, and it showed. There was no letterhead or style guide. Donors received poorly formatted appeal letters. Typos and grammatical errors were common in grants and corporate documents, and the copy written in brochures and on the website was dry and lifeless.

Had SVAS written about the good work they were doing in a compelling, professional manner, it may have been able to raise more money, secure more media coverage, attract more volunteers, and establish more business partnerships. Instead, the quality of writing was so poor and made so many negative impressions, it turned some people away from SVAS to more "professional" nonprofits in the area.

One of the first major ToDos the staff tackled after I took the helm at SVAS was evaluating corporate documents and marketing literature. The goal was to review each document and separate the poorly written ones from those of acceptable quality. After reviewing more than 200 documents, I'd say we tossed 90 percent into the dumpster and the remaining 10 percent went into a hopper to be rewritten and reformatted.

Later that week, staff started the arduous process of rewriting and reformatting the documents we kept and creating new versions of the ones we trashed. The objective was to write compelling collateral material to rebuild our brand, increase public awareness, raise money, and improve donor and volunteer relations.

The first thing we did was establish a comprehensive style guide. We then wrote a new set of marketing materials, programming literature, operational handbooks, and appeal letters to donors and foundations. Nothing was untouched; we even scrapped the website and built a new one.

Next, each staff member made a personal commitment to write better. They began to focus on spelling and grammar, and writing compelling, thoughtful copy. Staff also helped one another write and edit material. In fact, we created a policy stating at least three staff members had to proofread any document slated for public distribution.

It didn't take long for SVAS to see quality writing pay off. Within six months, executives from major media companies such as CNN, NBC, and Newsweek were responding to our compelling press releases with calls to produce features about the work we were doing to rehabilitate wounded veterans.

Newspaper columnists and talk show hosts called for interviews after reading our poignant op-ed pieces. Donors commented on our thoughtful appeal letters and inspiring support material. We even received compliments from foundations saying the quality of our grant applications and reports were some of the best they had ever seen.

Looking back, I believe one of the important factors that catapulted SVAS to national prominence, and one of the most understated, was SVAS' ability to write and publish all types of powerful and compelling material about our amazing programs and the impact we were having on people's lives.

If you want to bolt past the competition, fulfill your mission, and become a gold standard nonprofit, you must become a master wordsmith. The sooner in your lifecycle you make a commitment to this objective, the faster you'll see the results you hope to achieve.

Tactics and Tips
Hire staff who can write

When hiring staff, I seek out candidates who write well, especially managers. I want a program director who can write compelling stories about the experiences of our participants. I want a volunteer coordinator who can write inspiring thank-you notes, and I want a development officer who can write thoughtful appeal letters to donors.

Good writing requires good writers, and the more quality writers you have on staff—and on your board—the more opportunities you'll have to use the power and influence of writing to accomplish your objectives.

If you're a startup, you're in luck. You have a chance to a hire a team of good writers from the start. During the hiring process, make the skill of writing a top requirement for all positions.

At many nonprofits, the skill of writing is an afterthought in the hiring process. If you look at the job descriptions they post, the skill of writing is usually listed toward the bottom, or it's lumped into a general category such as "good communication skills."

That won't cut it. The skill of writing should be toward the top of every job description you post, including those for part-time positions. You should also include the skill of writing as one of your screens throughout the hiring process.

Carefully read emails and resumés of applicants and look for telling clues. Is their writing clear and concise? Is the tone of their writing professional and friendly? Do you spot spelling errors and sentence fragments? Do thoughts and ideas flow smoothly, or do they bounce around? Is the text well formatted?

If an applicant gets an interview, ask him or her to bring along a few writing samples. If you're hiring a grant writer, request samples of grants he's written. If you're hiring an operations manager, request samples of strategic plans, program assessments, board reports, or other documents she's written.

Read these documents carefully. How's the grammar? Spelling? Thought flow? Paragraph length? Layout and design?

When applicants make it to the final round of the interviewing process, give them a topic in their area of expertise and ask them to write three short paragraphs about it. Provide them a quiet room and a time limit, say 20 minutes. We all write better when we have time to edit and massage our writing, but writing on the spot, under a little pressure, is a telltale sign of someone's writing ability.

If forced to make a decision between two final applicants, a good writing sample might be the determining factor that swings your favor to one applicant over another.

Encourage staff to improve their writing

Let's say you're beyond the startup stage. You've been up and running for seven years and have 10 staff members. Four are poor writers, five are average, and one is an excellent writer. In this situation, you would want to find ways to improve the abilities of the less skilled writers.

This is easier said than done. The topic of writing can be a touchy subject because many people are insecure about their poor writing skills. They may have grown up in a grade school that didn't emphasize writing, or perhaps they were simply left-brained, science and math types.

So, if you're going to discuss someone's writing ability with them, be sensitive to their insecurities. I would also suggest keeping the discussion centered on improving the overall quality of writing by your nonprofit, not the poor writing skills of the person you're talking with. Make the focus corporate, not personal.

The good news is your staff can improve the quality of their writing with a little time and effort. Start simple. Suggest staff subscribe to a daily email subscription service such as "Spelling tip of the day," "Grammar tip of the day," or "Writing tip of the day." These are fun and gradual ways to improve writing skills.

You can also buy a subscription to Writer's Digest and leave it on a table in your break room. The magazine is loaded with tips on style, technique, grammar, and inspiration. The articles and sidebars are short and easy to understand.

One of the best ways to improve the writing quality of your staff is to get them to write more often. Encourage staff to take on assignments that require writing. Do you need a new brochure? How about a new page on your blog, a helpful report for the board, or a series of press releases? Does the thank-you letter to donors need updating? Would volunteers benefit from a training manual?

Assign these tasks to various staff or teams of staff. If you're fortunate to have a star writer on staff, use this person as a resource to help others improve their writing abilities as they work on their writing assignments.

Your star writer can also help fellow staff members learn how to organize thoughts, write compelling stories, and write with rhythm so words glide across the page. They can share samples of their writing to illustrate key concepts such as simplicity and clarity, and they can teach tips on editing and proofreading.

Writing is an art people can do well if they practice. Your job is to discover ways to create an easy-going environment that encourages your entire staff to become better writers. If you do, the written word will become a tool of power and influence your nonprofit can use to achieve the impossible.

Use a professional
You may find yourself in the unfortunate position of having talented and hardworking staff with little or no ability to write compelling copy and no motivation or willingness to learn. In this case, you need to outsource important writing tasks to a professional writer.

You have many choices. Freelance writers are always looking for work and most have affordable rates. Reporters at small newspapers or online periodicals often moonlight and may offer to write at discounted rates if they believe in your cause. Colleges and vocational schools have interns that will write for free because they can earn credit. Other options include professors or high school English teachers that teach writing, or one of your volunteers who has a writing background.

What's most important is finding an experienced writer who can quickly and affordably create powerful and effective copy. In some cases, a written document may be your only chance to raise money from a potential donor, persuade a decision maker, or influence a business partner. If you don't have good writers on staff to deliver the goods, outsource the work. Otherwise, potential opportunities will slip by one-by-one until there are none.

Editing – turn gold dust into gold bullion

The best writers know there is no such thing as good writing, just good rewriting. Rewriting (editing) is often crowned as the "art" of writing and it's usually the most time-consuming and frustrating aspect of writing.

I agree. I wrote the draft of this book in less than a month, but spent almost a year fine-tuning sentences, finding the right transitional phrases, swapping out dull words with sharp ones, and scanning for grammatical errors and typos. Editing can be a mind-numbing task and there were times I threw up my hands and said, "Why am I spending so much time on this?!"

You may not have a staff of great writers, but you may have a staff of great thinkers. An alternative to hiring a professional writer is having your staff write draft copies of your most important written material and then giving these documents to a professional editor that can transform gold dust into gold bullion.

A big advantage of taking this route is cost. Hiring an editor to edit copy is less expensive than hiring someone to write *and* edit copy. Plus, your staff knows your programs and operations better than anyone, so they are in the best position to write about such subjects.

Another option is to pay your star writers small bonuses for editing copy or teaching staff how to edit and polish writing. They could show staff why it's useful to read copy slowly out loud during the editing process to listen for rhythm and spot grammatical errors. They could explain why it's effective to sprinkle copy with quotes, anecdotes, and photographs, and why it's important to use generous amounts of white space.

Whoever you use to write copy, make sure quality editing is a part of the process because it's during the editing process that the real gems of what you want to say are made to shine the brightest.

Write compelling stories

Whether you're writing a letter to a donor or a press release for the local newspaper or blog, you can add tremendous power and effectiveness to your writing by adding compelling stories and anecdotes.

For example, let's say you want to write a blurb in your annual report about how your ski program enriched the lives of local children with disabilities during the past season. One way to do this is to list your accomplishments. You could display a bullet-pointed list highlighting how the program doubled the amount of children it served, tripled the amount of time each child skied, increased the amount of one-on-one instruction, and how the program taught three children with Down syndrome how to ski for the first time.

Pretty good, but bland. Now, imagine if you supplemented those facts with a success story about one of the children in your program, say Stu. Stu has Down syndrome, a heart condition, weak muscles, and a tendency to isolate himself. Stu had never attended your ski program because his family is poor and his mother thought the program cost a lot of money.

Early that December, Stu's mom bumped into one of your volunteers at the grocery store. During conversation, Stu's mom asked about the cost of the program and the volunteer assured her the ski program was free. The next week, with encouragement from the volunteer, Stu's mom brought Stu to one of your after-school ski clinics to see if he'd enjoy it.

By the end of the session, Stu was hooked. He joined the program and skied twice a week—all free. At the end of the season, he competed in a regional Special Olympics alpine racing event. He was a little shaky on the first run, but on the second run, Stu's time was good enough to earn him a silver medal. (You show a picture of Stu and his glorious smile holding his silver medal above his head on the winner's podium.)

Below the picture, you add a quote from Stu's mom. In it, she expresses gratitude for the program and how Stu would not have been able to participate in such a program had the program not been free. You end the story with a "kicker" stating how much time Stu has been spending in the gym lifting weights and training, because his new dream is to win a medal at next year's national Special Olympics alpine event.

Which was more compelling, the list of facts, or the story with the photo? Stories are powerful and persuasive vehicles that can bring your mission to life in the hearts and minds of all types of supporters.

Write more success stories of the great work you're doing. Write them in a compelling manner, accompanied by captivating photos, and distribute them through a variety of media channels. It's one of the simplest things you can do to motivate others to join and support your mission.

Takeaways

Your volunteer coordinator writes training manuals. Your board secretary writes fundraising invitations. Your marketing coordinator writes ad copy. Your board members write thank-you letters, and your chief executive writes partnership proposals. Everyone at your nonprofit has his or her hand in the writing jar.

Dull, choppy, and sloppy writing will smudge your image, taint your brand, and create negative impressions that steer people away from your nonprofit. Sharp, smooth, and clean writing will create positive, lasting impressions that draw people to your nonprofit.

If you want to separate yourself from the thousands of ordinary nonprofits fumbling about, it's important you realize, and put into practice, the power of quality writing and the ability it has to shape images, raise money, inspire people, and influence opinion.

Start by making quality writing a top priority at your nonprofit. Create standards and guidelines for quality writing and then set up structures to facilitate quality writing among staff.

Encourage staff to write compelling and persuasive text and give them the time to edit, massage, and rewrite documents. When hiring staff, make the skill of writing a primary job qualification. If you lack a team of good writers, outsource the work to professionals, or at least outsource the editing portions.

Quality writing is one of the secrets of success that flies under the radar of most nonprofit leaders. Don't miss this opportunity. Push quality writing to the forefront of your strategic ToDo list as early in your lifecycle as possible. If you do, you'll stand out from your competitors like a bestselling hardcover stands out against a secondhand book collecting dust on a discount rack.

CHAPTER 5

Public Speaking
Embracing opportunities to fearlessly share your good news

Whether or not we consider ourselves good speakers, we're all tuned in to people who speak well and those who don't. We get annoyed with "talkers" at cocktail parties. We dread boring seminar speakers, and we wince at long-winded speeches filled with "ums" and "ahs."

On the other hand, we admire good speakers. They make us smile. They give us goose bumps. They inspire us to join a cause, persuade us to change our opinion, and motivate us to write checks. Everyone loves a good speech—we just hope someone doesn't ask us to give one! We'd rather hide in a closet.

Public speaking is part of everyday life at a nonprofit. Program managers teach new staff, volunteer coordinators train volunteers, chief executives make fundraising speeches, and board members speak to community service organizations. Everyone answers phones, greets visitors, and talks about his or her favorite nonprofit around town.

Why is public speaking important?
Public speaking is a *First Things First* principle because speaking is the communication vehicle used most often to share information. A nonprofit whose staff and board are made up of good speakers has a distinct competitive advantage because so many nonprofits shy away from speaking opportunities—internally and publicly.

Anyone who has attended a major fundraising event knows the success of an event often depends on a keynote speaker's ability to inspire the audience, an auctioneer's ability to motivate donors to give, a chief executive's ability to talk passionately about an organization, and a participant's ability to share her experience.

The ability of a chief executive to give a great speech or compelling interview is essential, but more important is the ability of staff and board members to speak well in their given roles.

Effective speech at *every* level of nonprofit operations improves work productivity and efficiency, and we all know a business functions best when communication is clearly spoken and clearly understood.

Effective public speaking can also improve your nonprofit's image. Your staff and board are front and center in the community. The better they can communicate the great work you're doing and the impact you're making, the greater the likelihood they will win the hearts and minds of people they talk with, while earning respect and credibility for your nonprofit.

A great speech by a board chair may incite dozens of people to action, and something as simple as a friendly, two-minute phone call between your office manager and a donor may make a profound impression that transforms a minor donor into a major one.

Effective speaking, like effective writing, is another secret of success that flies under the radar of most nonprofits. Smart leaders of gold standard nonprofits know it's a tool of tremendous power and influence, and use it strategically to accomplish their objectives and fulfill their mission.

Be wise and do the same. Make effective speaking and public speaking top priorities at your nonprofit, and start applying the tactics of both the day you open for business. First things first!

Case Study: Breaking the spell
The fear of public speaking is very real for most people. For some, the thought of speaking in front of 10 people can ignite a cold sweat, cause a 20-point spike in blood pressure, and paralyze the ability to think.

Mary was one such person. She worked as a college intern at Sun Valley Adaptive Sports doing office work and running errands. One-on-one, Mary was friendly, easy-going, and a good conversationalist.

However, if you called on her to answer a question or provide an opinion in a group setting, she would tighten up and words would tumble from her lips like ice cubes.

I sat down with Mary after work one day and asked why she was so nervous to speak in group settings, even small ones with teammates. Mary then shared a heart-wrenching childhood story of an abusive relative who would ask questions about her homework; if Mary gave the wrong answer, he would scold her—sometimes physically.

A painful association with speaking like this would make anyone fearful of speaking in public. Mary went on to tell me her fear of public speaking was no longer connected to the fear of being scolded, but rather the fear of being judged for saying the wrong thing. "If I say something others don't agree with—they'll think I'm stupid!"

This is a powerful fear and we've all experienced it. Mary's explanation helped me understand why she was nervous about public speaking, but I was more curious to discover why she could speak with such ease and comfort in one-on-one situations. Mary said she was able to speak confidently in personal settings because she felt "safe." That is, when Mary talked with people she knew and trusted, she felt respected and felt no risk of judgment for what she might say or not say.

At the end of our chat, Mary told me she wanted to improve her public speaking skills. Over the next three months, I worked with her to develop a handful of strategies and tools to help her feel as comfortable and safe in small group settings as she did in one-on-one settings.

The primary strategy was simple: get Mary to participate in small group (safe) discussions with one to three people she knew and trusted, and then slowly increase the audience size as she increased her confidence and safety levels.

By the end of the year, after a lot of work and dedication, Mary was leading small team meetings. She spoke with conviction and ease, and her sentences flowed effortlessly. Mary said her big realization was learning she was entitled to her opinions, thoughts, and feelings. If people disagreed with what she said, it did not mean they disliked her or thought she was stupid.

One day, a television reporter popped into our offices. He heard Mary had been volunteering 10 hours a week for eight years (since junior high) at a shelter, where she helped cook meals for battered wives and abused children. The reporter asked if Mary would do an interview and share her experience. A year earlier, a question like this would have frozen Mary stiff and she would have cowered from the opportunity.

Instead, she accepted the offer with a smile. A week later, the entire staff huddled around a television and watched Mary give an inspiring account about how people can transcend the pain and scars of their youth and transform misfortunes into acts of service for those in need. The four-minute interview was so powerful and moving, the station played the spot three days in a row during primetime.

The interview was a pivotal experience for Mary. When she returned to the office after the interview, she was gabbing and chatting like a giddy old lady in a hair salon. The spell was broken.

Tactics and Tips
Everyone is a spokesperson
Public speaking is not a task reserved for chief executives in order to raise money at fundraising galas. Staff, board members, and volunteers speak publicly every time they conduct a training session, talk with parents, teach children, call business partners, attend a jazz festival, or shop for groceries. Everyone is a spokesperson, and the better everyone can articulate what you do, the more effective your nonprofit will be at fulfilling its mission.

If you want to build a team of good speakers, people need to know what to say. I'm always looking for ways to encourage staff, board members, and volunteers to memorize mission statements, recite core values, read collateral material, and understand program functions. Staff may be busy running programs and managing operations, but it's important they not forget the pillars on which their nonprofit stands.

Sharpen the knowledge of your staff, board members, and volunteers by providing time at meetings and training sessions to share information and answer questions. Explain the budgeting process or share the outcomes of the last board meeting. Discuss the latest changes to programming and how it will affect volunteer scheduling.

No matter what you discuss, remember the goal is to encourage the people connected with your nonprofit to learn more about how and why it operates the way it does so they can confidently share what they know with others.

Role-playing and coaching are two other ways to improve speaking skills. At random times ask staff and volunteers to recite your mission or core values, or ask someone to give an overview of the work they do, program they oversee, or an operational function they perform.

If you have inexperienced fundraising staff, sit in on some of their donor calls, so you can listen to the conversation and coach them on phone etiquette, selling techniques, tone, and timing.

It's every board member's responsibility to be a spokesperson. You'll want to make sure they understand the important aspects of programming, operations, and fundraising, so they can share this information with friends and business associates at parties, social outings, and community functions. Question and answer sessions and role-playing are just as useful for board members as they are for staff and volunteers, even more so in some cases.

Everyone connected with your nonprofit should be a spokesperson for the noble work you're doing. Your job is to teach them what to say and to provide frequent and safe opportunities for them to practice what to say—and what not to say—and how to say it. You also want to encourage everyone to joyfully and actively *share* what they know as they go about their daily lives in the community.

Seek out speaking opportunities
One way to differentiate your nonprofit from others is to seek out and embrace speaking opportunities, not avoid them. Community service organizations and local media are constantly looking for good speakers to share compelling stories and information of quality service work being done in the community.

You'll secure plenty of speaking engagements just by picking up the phone and calling your local Rotary and asking to speak, or calling a local radio station or online talk show host and making yourself available for an interview. If the interview goes well, you won't have to call them for a return visit; they'll be calling you.

As staff improves their public speaking skills, provide opportunities for them to speak at larger venues. Encourage different staff members to lead weekly staff meetings. During volunteer training sessions, invite staff members from different departments to talk about the jobs they perform and the primary functions of their departments. Participate in public outreach opportunities such as concerts, benefits, fairs, or fun runs where you can showcase your mission, and staff and board members can talk about what you do and ways to get involved.

You should also encourage selected staff to set up television, radio, and newspaper interviews. Ask managers to attend board meetings to present program and operation updates, and require your chief executive and program managers to make a certain number of presentations and public speeches each year.

If you have board members who enjoy public speaking, arrange opportunities for them to speak to community service organizations such as the American Legion, Lions Club, and Jaycees.

Slow and easy

Almost everyone has some level of fear and anxiety when speaking to large groups, important people, or on camera. It's natural. As you help staff and board members improve their speaking skills, you'll want to be sensitive to the pace at which you increase their comfort levels, so they learn to welcome more challenging speaking opportunities, not repel them.

Start slowly and easily. Assess everyone's comfort level and then establish a customized plan to improve each person's speaking skills based on each person's desire and motivation to improve his or her skills and your needs to improve the overall speaking skills of your nonprofit.

If you're serious about improving the speaking skills of those connected with your nonprofit, you'll need to make room in your budget to pay for it. Allocate funds for books, classes, and webinars. If some of your staff want to join the local chapter of Toastmasters, pay their annual membership dues. Let everyone know you're committed to support quality speaking as much as you expect them to improve their speaking ability.

Prepare, prepare, prepare

Great speakers prepare. They study their topic and audience, make notes, and practice giving their speech dozens of times before they deliver it live.

The best advice you can give your staff, volunteers, and board members about public speaking is to let them know how important it is to prepare.

The more they prepare for a speaking engagement the more effective and comfortable they will be. This holds true whether they are holding a meeting with three staff or making a fundraising speech to 300 donors.

Here are seven tactics every speaker should use to prepare for any type of speaking engagement:

1. *Be yourself.* Good speakers must be authentic to sound credible. This means they need to be themselves. Everyone has his or her own natural style of speaking. Some people are soft spoken and personal; others are loud and charismatic. Develop a speaking style that lets your personality shine through.

2. *Stick to the basics.* Experienced public speakers use a handful of basic speaking techniques they know resonate with all audiences. They speak clearly, tell compelling and funny stories, and exhibit a comfortable and confident stage presence. They also know it's important to be positive, genuine, honest, inspiring, passionate, and interesting.

3. *Know the audience.* Effective speakers study their audiences long before making a speech. They want to know everything they can about the people they are speaking to so they can tailor a speech that appeals to their beliefs, expectations, level of education, and extent of knowledge about the subject matter. The better you can do this, the more effective your speeches will be.

4. *Have a specific message and theme in mind.* Rambling thoughts and senseless tangents will confuse an audience. You must have a clear idea what you want to say and why you think it's important and relevant to your audience. What is the purpose of your speech? What can you say to inspire the audience? What three things do you want the audience to remember from your speech?

5. *Practice, practice, and then practice some more.* Great speakers practice their speeches out loud. They practice standing up and they practice in front of others. For a big speech, start practicing three weeks ahead of time. Never wing-it. When practicing at home, stand in the center of your living room and gesture to lamps and other items, pretending they're your audience. It's

also a good idea to experiment with pitch and cadence as you practice.

6. *Use note cards.* Memorizing a speech is very difficult. Delivering a memorized speech can sound flat, unless the speaker has years of experience making memorized speeches. Reading a detailed speech from full-length text can sound just as dry as a memorized speech. It can force you to spend too much time reading a speech instead of making eye contact with your audience.

The solution? Note cards. Short phrases from key points in a speech can prompt you with enough information to allow you to speak freely about the topics you're sharing. Note cards also act as mini outlines and can help you flow smoothly from one topic to the next.

7. *Get comfortable.* Public speaking makes even the most seasoned speakers a little nervous. This is common, but great speakers know they will be most effective if they feel comfortable and confident.

Every speaker must find a technique that transforms nervous energy into relaxed confidence. It helps to breathe deeply before you start speaking and during pauses in a speech. You may also find it relaxing to gesture with your hands during a speech and take time to smile at your audience.

Takeaways

You may be able to hide from writing, but you cannot hide from speaking. It surrounds everyone, every day, all day. Nonprofits that fail to communicate effectively have difficulty raising money, motivating others, and growing. They slip into the background and remain miles short of their potential.

If you want to become a gold standard nonprofit, you need to assemble a team of staff, board members, and volunteers who speak effectively and are willing to seek out public speaking opportunities on a regular basis. If you do, you will build trust and credibility in your community, influence and motivate people, differentiate from the competition, develop remarkable programs, and raise a lot of money.

To build a team of effective speakers, start by making effective speaking a top priority early on. Hire staff and nominate board members with public speaking experience and strong speaking skills, and keep everyone's speaking skills sharp by providing well-funded training and practice opportunities.

Everyone connected with your nonprofit is a potential spokesperson. Once you have a team of confident, effective speakers, seek out public speaking opportunities to get as many of them involved as possible. They're contributing to the amazing work you're doing and making a difference, so find ways for them to publicly share the good news!

Don't kid yourself. It's a dog-eat-dog world out there for nonprofits, and those who bark best get most of the treats and attention.

CHAPTER 6

Chief Executive

*Hiring or developing a social entrepreneur
superhero to do the impossible*

There are few decisions more important than the one you'll make when hiring a chief executive. A good chief executive can set the stage for growth and sustainability. A great chief executive can propel a nonprofit to places it never dreamed, inspire a community, and transform an industry. A chief executive can also be a nonprofit's worst nightmare. He can destroy morale, squander funds, offend donors, and run a nonprofit into the ground.

Every board has the best intentions when hiring a chief executive. It wants to hire the most qualified candidate who will fulfill the mission and fit snugly into the culture.

To accomplish this, boards sift through dozens of qualifying attributes. They consider experience, education, and motivation. They examine a candidate's ability to lead, raise money, overcome obstacles, and manage staff, and they look for a track record of success and a history of healthy relationships with former boards.

These qualifying attributes, and many others, are important factors to consider. That's a given. The mistake most nonprofit boards make when hiring a chief executive is placing too much emphasis on the skills and experience a candidate possesses and too little emphasis on the *nature* of the candidate.

This is why the single most important attribute a board should be looking for in a chief executive is the attribute of *social entrepreneurialism*.

I say this because the majority of skills, drive, energy, and experience needed for a nonprofit to succeed are found naturally and abundantly in a chief executive who lives and breathes the principles of social entrepreneurialism—the social entrepreneur.

Why is it important to hire or develop a social entrepreneur as a chief executive?

Nonprofits typically face enormous challenges and limited resources in their efforts to develop infrastructure, run programs, raise money, and manage people.

Hiring—or developing—a social entrepreneur as a chief executive is a *First Things First* principle because social entrepreneurs typically have the best skill sets and personalities required to manage intense, high-pressure environments like those found at many nonprofits. They thrive on stress, change, and diversity. They enjoy the challenge of tackling large-scale social problems and the tireless hours required to solve them.

Boards of nonprofits rarely hire or develop social entrepreneurs because they don't know what a social entrepreneur is, or understand the value a social entrepreneur can provide.

As I said, the focus of most boards is to hire someone with industry experience and a skill set that matches the programming characteristics of their nonprofit. "We're in the adaptive sports industry, so let's hire a chief executive with a strong background in recreation therapy or physical therapy."

Industry and programming experience is useful, but the ability to understand business, raise money, motivate staff, develop partnerships, craft solutions, facilitate grassroots advocacy, and manage hundreds of other non-programming tasks has little to do with whether or not a chief executive can teach children with autism how to snowboard.

The truth is a talented, experienced social entrepreneur can run just about *any* nonprofit. Social entrepreneurs are driven by excellence and performance and it's their nature to fully immerse themselves in whatever they do. They quickly become experts in the industries in which they work, and overcome obstacles in their way as they march with enthusiasm to fulfill a mission and inspire people along the way.

One of the wisest decisions your nonprofit can make is to hire or develop a social entrepreneur as your chief executive as early as possible in your lifecycle—one who can best run your organization, not your programs. First things first!

Case Study: Making the unintuitive decision

When I started working with Sun Valley Adaptive Sports, I knew little or nothing about cerebral palsy, Asperger's syndrome, Tourette's syndrome, traumatic brain injuries, or blindness. I had no rehabilitation experience, no therapy degree, and no experience in the military. The only experience I had working with people with disabilities was the short time I spent dating a woman with paraplegia when I was 33.

The SVAS board did not hire me because of my experience in the adaptive sports industry. I had none. They hired me because I had a 20-year track record of building and operating gold standard nonprofits and businesses, and a reputation for quickly transforming rags into riches and dreams into realities.

The board saw my diverse background and experience as a benefit, not a liability. I had experience as a nonprofit founder, board chair, chief executive, and major donor. I had raised millions in venture capital for startup software companies and millions for startup nonprofit organizations. I had managed teams with MBAs to build corporations and teams of interns to launch nonprofits.

I had studied finance and marketing, as well as computer science and journalism. I had helped build a large for-profit company that designed software for Fortune 500 companies, and founded a small nonprofit that fed hungry children. I had worked with engaged boards and disengaged boards, and I had worked in cultures where staff wore business suits and cultures where staff wore flip-flops.

I'm grateful the SVAS board was looking to hire a social entrepreneur and believed only a social entrepreneur had the skills and variety of experiences needed to raise SVAS from the rubble that buried it. I accepted the board's offer to hire me in the fall of 2005 and promised to transform SVAS into a nonprofit of national prominence in three to five years.

Four years later, SVAS became a Cinderella story: a small nonprofit that was once hanging on the threads of survival had become a nationally recognized name in the adaptive sports industry with plans of building the nation's largest nonmedical rehabilitation center for wounded veterans with traumatic brain injuries and post-traumatic stress disorder.

Our rapid and astounding success was the culmination of talented staff, dozens of passionate volunteers, and hundreds of gracious supporters and business partners. My contribution was providing the skills, drive, and experience of a social entrepreneur, and to cast a vision and see to it we fulfilled it in the most efficient, effective, and meaningful manner.

Any number of talented social entrepreneurs could have done what I did for SVAS. Like me, they would have brought a specific set of social entrepreneurial skills and experience to provide the knowledge, enthusiasm, and discernment SVAS needed to anticipate changes, dodge mistakes, seize opportunities, and lead with a sense of purpose that comes only from years of hard work and having a variety of successes and failures.

One of the smartest things you can do as a nonprofit is to let go of the notion that you must hire a chief executive with industry experience. Industry experience is useful, but it's not nearly as important as social entrepreneurial experience—not even close.

If you want a chief executive who can deliver the goods beyond expectation, find yourself a social entrepreneur who has a passion for your mission, fits your culture, embodies the principles of social entrepreneurialism, and has an exemplary track record of success. It's not an intuitive decision to make, but it will prove to be one of your wisest.

If you already have a chief executive, it's important that your board invest in his professional development. Why? Because if you're like many nonprofits, you have a small budget and small budgets cannot afford highly skilled and experienced chief executives.

This leaves many nonprofits in a quandary. On one hand, they need a high-performance chief executive with the skills and experience required to build a high-performance nonprofit. On the other hand, they typically lack the funds needed to hire a high-performance executive.

If your nonprofit is in this position, and you believe your current chief executive has the ability and desire to become a high-performance executive, encourage your board to emotionally and financially support his professional development. It may turn out to be the best investment your board ever makes.

Tactics and Tips

If you're hiring a chief executive, what attributes do you look for? If you're mentoring one, what attributes should you develop? No executive will possess all the following social entrepreneur attributes, but the best ones will possess traits from most of them. Use the following paragraphs as a checklist during your hiring and development process.

Moral skills

You need to hire or develop a social entrepreneur driven by a moral compass; someone who genuinely cares about people and the organization. He will have a big heart. He will do the right thing because it's the right thing to do, not because he feels he has to, or because it will appease someone or comply with a law.

Attributes: Humility. Honesty. Integrity. Fairness. Inclusiveness. Respectfulness. Genuineness. Compassion. Gratefulness. Strongly believes in ethics and transparency. Takes responsibility and ownership. Never passes the buck or blames others. Exhibits overflowing love, kindness, and justice.

Drive skills

Social entrepreneurs deliver the goods. No obstacle is too daunting. They thrive on making things happen and they strive to achieve big goals and lofty visions with limited resources. Give them an impossible task and they smile.

A resumé of work related success is not good enough. You need to find a social entrepreneur with success stories in all areas of life. Great social entrepreneurs do just about everything well—it's their nature. They are doers. They work hard. They never say never. They endeavor to achieve great heights in all they do. They like to win. To them, the glass is always half full.

Attributes: Persistence. Perseverance. Resiliency. Inquisitiveness. Record-breaking productivity. High achiever. Insatiable learner. Innovative. Proactive. Calculated risk taker. Follows through.

Communication skills

Great social entrepreneurs are master communicators. They understand the importance of motivating others to join their cause, support it, and propel it. They can give a great speech, champion a new initiative, and sell ice to Eskimos. They are savvy promoters of their organizations and themselves.

Attributes: Exceptional understanding of all marketing functions including publicity, promotion, public relations, advertising, and sales. Dynamic speaker. Gifted writer. Good listener. Enthusiastic promoter. Great collaborator. Avid user of technology.

Leadership skills

Social entrepreneurs lead. They take initiative and have an uncanny ability to visualize the future and pull others along. They are servant leaders that lead by example, not by bossing people around. They successfully manage through dark and challenging times. They humbly manage the spotlight without seeking it.

Attributes: Decisiveness. Wisdom. Courage. Flexibility. Accountability. Responsibility. Selflessness. Humility. Enterprising. Thinks before reacting. Calm under pressure and stress. Ability to inspire and influence. Desire to empower others.

People skills

When you distill business to its essence, most executives will tell you it's about people and relationships. There are donors to meet, staff to manage, volunteers to motivate, participants to help, and business partners to persuade. Your chief executive will be the voice and face of your nonprofit, so it's important you hire or develop someone who gets along with all types of people in a variety of situations. He should be likeable and approachable and an aura of positive energy should surround him.

Attributes: Friendliness. Sincerity. Patience. Motivating. Loyalty. Eternal encourager. Inspiring. Magnetic. Treats people with equality and respect. Regularly offers praise and gratitude. Seeks ways to collaborate. Listens attentively. Always willing to lend a hand.

Business skills

The best social entrepreneurs possess a broad range of business skills and can tackle any job. You want a chief executive who can fulfill the needs of your nonprofit *and* fits snuggly into your culture. You'll also want an executive who is both a competent theorist and a competent practitioner. Meaning, he will have a track record of *habitually* creating and innovating visions of value, but will also have the skills, temperament, and experience to transform visions into reality.

Attributes: Competent and experienced in the primary areas of business including marketing, administration, fundraising, operations, programming, accounting, finance, technology, governance, human resources, and risk management. Quick learner. Skilled networker. Seeks counsel and the opinion of others. Accepts criticism. Uncanny ability to quickly solve difficult problems. Jack of many trades.

Efficiency and effectiveness skills

Social entrepreneurs give attention to the right things. This is effectiveness. They also know how to do the right things in the right manner. This is efficiency. They are maestros at managing the efficient and effective use of limited resources and then directing them toward the right operational and programming realities for today's needs and tomorrow's vision.

Attributes: Frugality. Master organizer. Motivated by performance and outcomes. A healthy balance of risk and reward. A thorough understanding of opportunity cost. Always looking for ways to improve and refine.

Stress management skills

Running a fast-growing nonprofit is stressful—often insanely stressful. Boards ask for unexpected reports. Computer networks crash. Income falls short of projections. Staff drama infects morale. Rainstorms cancel fundraising events. Foundations make last minute grant requests. Key managers quit unexpectedly. Bookkeepers embezzle funds. The list goes on.

Stress is part of daily life at nonprofits. The smaller the nonprofit and the faster its growth rate, the greater the chance stress will be part of daily business. Steer clear of candidates with short fuses and those who are habitually anxious, edgy, and tense. Look for social entrepreneurs who thrive on stressful situations, but remain composed and focused when dealing with them.

Attributes: Resiliency. Self-control. Confidence. Patience. Prudence. A sense of calm. Thinks before acting. Makes wise decisions and takes appropriate action in stressful situations. Has the ability to walk away from risky circumstances.

Takeaways

If you operate a fast-growing nonprofit, you must realize, truly realize, the Herculean tasks ahead of you. Work of this magnitude requires a specific skill set far beyond that of an executive with two years of industry experience and a good education.

What you need are the services of a talented and experienced social entrepreneur. Only he or she possesses the fiery passion, diverse talents, committed vision, seasoned experience, and inexhaustible determination to persist until the job is done—and to do it in a manner that exceeds all expectation.

By nature, social entrepreneurs are driven to excellence in everything they do. Their personal mission is to create tremendous value with limited time and resources. They're wired to do the right thing, in the right manner, for the right reason, and they are friendly, compassionate souls who energize and inspire those in their presence.

Don't delay. Hire or develop a social entrepreneur who has a passion for your mission, fits your culture, and exhibits the majority of attributes of a high-performance social entrepreneur. If you have an inexperienced executive in place that is unmotivated to learn and grow, it may be time to consider a replacement.

Without a social entrepreneur at the helm of your nonprofit, you might crawl along for years and fall far short of fulfilling your dreams and mission. Or worse, your chief executive might lead your nonprofit down a path of mediocrity from which it may not recover.

If you want to be a glittering gold standard nonprofit, you don't need to hire or develop Superman or Wonder Woman to fulfill your mission and achieve your dreams, but you will want to hire or develop a social entrepreneur superhero. The cape is optional.

CHAPTER 7

Executive-Board Relations

Dousing the ring of fire

Tension. Irritation. Frustration. These are three words often used by chief executives and board members to describe their relationship to each other. Not all executive-board relationships at nonprofits are contentious, but most could be much healthier and more productive.

For a nonprofit to thrive, it must develop a systematic approach of creating and sustaining a healthy executive-board relationship, as well as methods of solving relationship issues when they arise.

You can trace much of the strife between boards and chief executives to unmet expectations. Boards get frustrated because chief executives can be lone wolves with big egos who like to push agendas without board support. It also annoys boards when executives make major decisions without informing the board, or when executives withhold information from the board, especially when it's negative.

Executives get just as frustrated with board members. Irritation reaches boiling proportions when board members blow off meetings with no reason, vote on changes to programs they have never seen, drive personal agendas, micromanage staff, fail to make annual contributions, and make policy changes without considering the implications to operations, programming, or staff workload.

Boards are also notorious for ignoring their responsibilities to raise funds, recruit board members, and volunteer for programs. Most board members of small nonprofits have little or no board experience, yet often act with a sense of entitlement. To a seasoned chief executive with good intentions, a board like this feels like a hangnail.

Why are executive-board relations important?

Maintaining a healthy relationship between a chief executive and a board of directors is a *First Things First* principle because the relationship between the two sets the tone for a nonprofit's culture and productivity—inside and outside the organization.

A healthy executive-board relationship is friendly, collegial, professional, and productive. It's team oriented and cloaked with respect, admiration, and authentic passion. The result emits positive energy and enthusiasm to the staff, volunteers, and the community. When this type of relationship is in place, it creates a dynamic and inspiring work environment that transforms a "you" and "I" nonprofit into a "we" nonprofit.

On the other hand, a contentious, bitter executive-board relationship can rot the drive and enthusiasm of everyone. This often leads to hundreds of hours of lost productivity as the nonprofit must divert its energy and resources to grind through conflicts. Every hour spent dealing with a nagging issue could be spent raising money and executing the mission. Fun becomes resented "work." Interest withers. Passion wanes and everyone mumbles, "I didn't sign up for this! I don't need the headache and aggravation."

If a chief executive and a board of directors cannot get along and resolve their differences, the relationship will eventually become so corrosive that the nonprofit will lose favor and funding and it may take *years* to regain the position and momentum it once had.

This all may sound gloomy, but it's reality. If you have your sights set on becoming a gold standard nonprofit, you must, absolutely must, take action as early in your lifecycle as possible to ensure a healthy relationship exists between your chief executive and your board. First things first!

Case study: Digesting the truth

Weeks before I rescued Sun Valley Adaptive Sports, the relationship between the executive director and board of directors was volcanic. Months of tension and aggravation between the two—and between the executive and staff—led to an explosive, public confrontation where the executive, who founded the organization, threw his office keys at the board chair and said, "I quit!"

The board gladly accepted his resignation. It was a relief to some board members who felt he was in a role beyond his capabilities and experience. Most staff also sighed with relief. They felt unappreciated and uninspired, and said their suggestions fell on deaf ears as operations ran amok and programming became increasingly disorganized.

The executive director had his own beefs. He felt controlled by the board and felt like the board was meddling in the daily affairs of the business and doing too little to raise funds, volunteer, and find new board members.

The situation was a mess and it was my job as the new chief executive to diffuse the drama, renew morale, and rebuild the organization. There were many challenges to address and some of the biggest were the issues the former executive had with the board.

After six years of operation, the board had still not defined roles and responsibilities for its members. There were no governing policies, no committees, no strategic plan, no board development plan, and no board accountability.

Most of the board was apathetic. Only a few members out of 11 had nonprofit board experience. This would not have been a problem had the other board members been *willing* to learn what it means to be a best practices board member and work as a team to develop and fulfill the typical roles and responsibilities of board members.

Instead, members filled one board meeting after another with empty chatter about what *could* be done or *should* be done, but no one was willing to do the work that *needed* to be done. In the few instances when the board said it would produce a document or write policy, the responsibility inevitably fell on my shoulders because the board claimed it was too busy to complete the project, or said they didn't have the expertise.

I would have been fine with the board passing off an occasional project, but when my offers to help became their method of doing work, I felt used. This irritated me and eventually created tension between the board and me.

I also started to feel a little resentment toward the board because the staff was working seven days a week, month after month to rebuild and retool every operational structure and every program, while most of the board was doing very little to help rebuild the organization and even less to rebuild the board.

In fact, the more successful SVAS became, the more listless the board became. And why not, I was raising 98 percent of the money, programming was nationally acclaimed, and operations were humming. It felt as if the board was thinking, "Gee, the staff is doing such a great job, why do we need to do anything?"

I expressed my concerns many times to the board and to the board chair. In response, they nodded their heads in agreement, made a few hollow commitments, and repeated how great things were going. Of course, nothing would happen.

In my view, the board chair was partly responsible for the board's apathy. With no board chair experience, nominal nonprofit experience, and minimal time for board work, a lack of board leadership prevailed. As a result, the board seemed unmotivated to fulfill its responsibilities, uninspired to volunteer, and unwilling to be held accountable.

I'll never forget the meeting where one board member stood up and, speaking on behalf of the board said, "We feel staff are paid employees of the organization and are expected to do the work of the organization. Board members are volunteers of the organization and *should not be expected* to do any work, or be held accountable to fulfill any work related tasks."

I thought, "Whoa! What planet were they living on?" It was at that moment I realized the culture of the board and the culture of the staff were antipodal.

Discouraged and disappointed, I left the board meeting wondering why a group of people who claimed to be so committed to our mission were so unwilling to do the work needed to support it. It was a classic case of lip service passion.

In the fall of 2007, I suggested SVAS hire a facilitator to lead our strategic planning session. The board agreed. I asked the facilitator if she would spend a portion of the session talking about roles and responsibilities of board members and chief executives, and standards of best practices for board operations. With a third party offering advice and direction, my secret hope was the board would learn how a best practices board functions and how they should interact with a chief executive.

The planning session was a milestone for SVAS. The facilitator talked at length about what it means to be a best practices board member and the typical roles and responsibilities that go along with board membership. She covered fundraising obligations, fiscal responsibilities, policy development, committee participation, staff appreciation, board operations, volunteering, executive-board relations, meeting attendance, moral obligations, and micromanagement.

Over and over, the facilitator repeated how important it was for a board to be held accountable for its responsibilities, obligations, and commitments. The other point she frequently emphasized was how critical it was for a board and chief executive to work side-by-side to achieve the goals and fulfill the mission of a nonprofit.

The truth was too much to digest. Within a few months, most of the board members resigned, including the board chair. It was sudden and a bit traumatic, but purging the board turned out to be a seminal event in the history of SVAS.

It took more than six months to fill seven new positions and it was worth the wait. The new board members had long track records of nonprofit experience, active involvement, and had made exceptional contributions to the nonprofits they had worked with.

The new board chair was a fiery, corporate executive with decades of business and nonprofit experience, and had the backbone to hold board members accountable.

With a new board chair at the helm and a team of quality board members eager to work, the culture of the board changed overnight. Drama evaporated. Respect returned. Board meetings were fun and lively, members started volunteering regularly, and everyone was offering to help in whatever capacity they could.

By spring 2009, SVAS was soaring to unimaginable heights. In fact, things were going so well and we were growing so fast, the board and staff voted to explore the possibility of building a multi-million dollar rehabilitation center for our wounded veterans program. Four years earlier, the only thing the board and former executive director were exploring together was a lawsuit against each other.

The restoration of the SVAS board and its relationship with me is a testament to what a culture of hard-working, passionate people can accomplish when the executive-board relationship is healthy and working in partnership to achieve common goals.

The success of your nonprofit will be directly correlated to the quality of your executive-board relationship and how well you establish and nurture a healthy and productive relationship early on in your lifecycle.

Do not delay. Do what you need to do, as soon as you can, to establish a healthy relationship, even if it means making unpopular decisions and taking unpopular actions. The survival of your nonprofit depends on it.

Tactics and Tips
Equal but different roles – a philosophy
The first thing you need to do to build a healthy executive-board relationship is establish a *philosophy* about how the executive and board should view each other's roles.

I'm not talking about the details of who should be responsible for what; that comes later. I'm talking about a belief or philosophy your nonprofit holds about the executive-board relationship.

Some old-school boards have a top-down approach to management and see themselves as superior to chief executives because they see executives as "employees" with no voting rights.

Executives, on the other hand, often feel superior to board members, because most of the time they do the bulk of the work, raise the majority of funds, pick up the balls board members drop, and often have more nonprofit experience.

According to best practice standards, neither position is superior to the other. Rather, the chief executive and board should view their relationship as *collegial*. This means the chief executive and board are *equals*, though they have different roles and responsibilities.

At the very least, the executive-board relationship philosophy you adopt should include values of respect, admiration, and encouragement. It should also include working together in a collaborative, compassionate, and sacrificial manner to propel your nonprofit's mission.

You can tweak the values and beliefs any way you want, but what's most important is creating an executive-board relationship philosophy. Put this at the top of your corporate ToDo list. Once it's written and approved, add it to your bylaws and work it into your culture as soon as possible.

You should establish policies requiring the board to share this philosophy when orienting new board members, hiring a chief executive, and holding strategic planning sessions. This way, the philosophy will remain front and center in people's minds and in your nonprofit's culture.

Clearly defined roles and responsibilities
Unmet expectations and undefined roles and responsibilities are kindling for relationship fires. For the relationship between the chief executive and board to be a healthy and productive one, everyone needs to know who is responsible for what and who is responsible to whom.

To do this, you need to create a set of clearly defined expectations, roles, and responsibilities for the chief executive and the board. You must also establish terms of accountability, levels of participation requirements, and methods of evaluation. Discussing these topics can create tension and controversy because many executives and boards have no idea what nonprofit standards exist for such things, or they try injecting personal agendas.

If you have any suspicion your chief executive and board might fall into a contentious, unproductive discussion when developing terms and protocols for these governance items, I strongly suggest hiring an experienced mediator to facilitate the process. A good mediator can save everyone hours of bickering and weeks of lingering drama. If you're lucky, the process will turn out to be a fulfilling experience that deepens board culture and builds team spirit.

Below is a brief list of standard roles and responsibilities for chief executives and board members. There are others, but these will prove most useful for beginning the process of building or enriching a healthy executive-board relationship.

~ ~ ~

Roles and Responsibilities – Chief Executive
Establish a job description
You can't expect to hold a chief executive accountable for responsibilities if there are none. The most important thing a board can do to manage the roles, responsibilities, and expectations of a chief executive is to write a detailed job description.

A job description for a chief executive should cover all functional areas of business including financial, programming, operations, administration, fundraising, board reporting, and marketing. It should also cover responsibilities for employee oversight and board relations.

You'll want to design a job description detailed enough so your board can use it to manage your chief executive, but broad enough to prevent micromanagement. It's important that your board grant plenty of freedom to your executive so she can do her job without feeling as if a pack of overbearing parents is peering over her shoulder waiting to question every decision and monitor every action.

You'll also want to establish well-defined performance measures tied to the details of the job description. This way, your chief executive will have a clear understanding of what work to accomplish and what goals to achieve throughout the year, and the board will have standards by which to evaluate her performance.

Manage operations and staff
The primary responsibility of a chief executive is managing the day-to-day operations of the organization and overseeing staff. You hired a quality executive because you felt she was the best person for the job. It's the responsibility of the board to provide oversight of the work she performs, but it is not their responsibility to micromanage. It's a delicate balance indeed.

If the chief executive lacks the ability to do her job, or has the ability, but not the willingness, then you may need to let her go. After a few blowouts and patches, it's better to replace a flat tire than to repair it.

The primary guideposts for a nonprofit are its mission, vision, strategic plan, operational plan, fundraising plan, and budget. The executive typically works with the board to develop the first three of these items. For the second three, the executive typically develops drafts, presents them to the board for discussion and approval, and then executes them once the board votes to adopt them.

The board approves major employment policies and the funds to hire staff, but the process of hiring, managing, and firing staff is the responsibility of the chief executive. In small nonprofits, it's common courtesy to allow a few board members to meet senior level staff before they are hired, but the executive should have the authority to make the final call.

Inform the board

In the nonprofit world, the chain of command is clear: the chief executive is an employee of the organization and reports to the board. As part of her reporting duties, the chief executive is responsible for informing the board with regular updates covering all areas of operations, administration, programming, and finances.

I suggest the executive, in collaboration with key staff, write a brief, bullet-pointed "monthly update" covering the most recent highlights of the organization. She can send this update to board members prior to board meetings. These updates also provide a historical record of successes and challenges that management can use to design market-ing material, write annual reports, or to refer to during strategic plan-ning sessions.

Transparency equates to trust. For the relationship between the chief executive and board to be healthy and productive, executives must be willing and comfortable to share bad or unfortunate news.

I remember the time when one of our SVAS ski instructors collided with one of our participants during a lesson. The next morning, after the participant spent a night in the hospital, a lawyer called to say the family was filing a lawsuit.

A lawsuit had serious implications to SVAS and our board. After hanging up with the lawyer, I immediately phoned our board chair and explained the situation. Fortunately, one of our board members knew a renowned lawyer. We contacted him for advice. He called the partici-pant's lawyer. By the end of the day he resolved the situation and no legal action took place. Whew!

Stuff happens and boards understand. They want to help. In some cases it's their responsibility to help because boards are liable for instances of "gross negligence." Your chief executive should immediately inform your board if a senior manager quits, your largest donor decides not to make a gift, a legal issue arises, or a new partnership is underway that will change the way you deliver services.

Boards don't need to get involved with petty problems, but it's the responsibility of the chief executive to honestly and promptly inform the board of any *major* problems, changes, and potentially damaging situations.

Support the board

Board members range from billionaires who attended Harvard to single parents who dropped out of high school. Regardless of education and background, it's the chief executive's responsibility to help board members be effective.

The most respected chief executives provide the necessary leadership to engage, encourage, and inspire board members. They are always on the hunt for opportunities to help board members better serve the board and the organization.

It's also important that board members feel a sense of respect and gratitude from the chief executive. Board members might not admit it, but they do want to feel their time and contributions are valued and appreciated by the chief executive. This is why it's important for executives to make a special effort to spend one-on-one time with board members to thank them for their help and support.

Board participation

The chief executive is typically the leader of the organization and it's her responsibility to provide leadership, wisdom, and information at board meetings. She should sit on the board and be treated with the same respect and admiration as any other board member. This is the essence of the servant-leader role and why it's vital for the board and chief executive to foster a collegial relationship.

Even though chief executives sit on the board, they should not have board voting rights. In rare cases, boards grant chief executives voting rights, but I don't recommend this due to obvious conflicts. The term for this non-voting position on the board is called *ex officio*. It means, "by way of position," or "by right of office" the chief executive has rights to sit on the board. Most nonprofits include an *ex officio* statement in their bylaws to outline their executive's role on the board.

Although chief executives don't have the right to vote, the board should provide its executive the opportunity to cast an *ex officio* vote, or at least give her an opportunity to express her opinion and provide input on a topic or issue before the board casts its vote.

Boards and chief executives often squabble over who should prepare the board agenda. It's the responsibility of the chief executive to prepare and distribute board agendas with input from the board chair.

The chief executive and board chair should meet or talk before board meetings to discuss important agenda items in an effort to speak with a unified voice and avoid surprises. Even if the chief executive and board chair hold different positions, the board will feel more at ease knowing the chief executive and board chair discussed the agenda ahead of time.

One area of debate is who should lead board meetings—the board chair or chief executive? The board chair is more common, but the executive can be just as effective. Why? She typically knows the most about the operations, programming, and finances of the nonprofit. She also has good communication skills (or should) and is used to working with people and businesses in a collaborative effort to solve problems and discuss opportunities.

In the end, it's the board's call. However, if the chief executive runs board meetings, it's important she engage the board chair and board members in topics of discussion in a collaborative, collegial manner. Remember, board meetings are environments of democracy, not dictatorship.

Board member nomination and orientation
The chief executive should be responsible for taking an active role in the board nominating process. She is in the best position to know the needs of the nonprofit and the types of people who can best help it. She's also in a good position to recommend candidates because she's in constant and close interaction with community leaders, business partners, and donors.

It's important that potential board members have a good relationship with the chief executive and fit into the culture of the board, and to a lesser extent, the culture of the nonprofit. The chief executive and members of a nominating committee need to thoroughly screen board nominees. As I said earlier, you want to create strong filters and set expectations to ensure you bring on and retain high quality people.

This means finding candidates with track records of getting along with others in business and social settings. Call past employers, business partners, and nonprofits they've worked with. Are they team players? Are they good listeners? Are they interested in hearing the opinions of others? Do they shut down if they don't get their way? Do they seek common ground when negotiating? Are they sensitive to the feelings of others? Do they exhibit authentic passion or lip service passion?

Fast-tracking board nominees for any position without proper screening is a recipe for executive-board relationship calamity. Here's a piece of advice to keep in mind: Before you nominate—investigate!

Again, the goal is to build an effective board, not a contentious one. This starts with healthy, productive relationships between all the board members and, most importantly, a healthy relationship with the chief executive.

Once a board votes to approve a nominee to board membership, a board member or the board nominating committee should be responsible to orient new board members about their roles, responsibilities, and expectations of their work and time commitments.

The chief executive's responsibility in this process is to orient new board members about key areas of programming, planning, accounting, fundraising, and any other areas that will help new board members understand the structure and operations of the nonprofit.

~ ~ ~

Roles and Responsibilities – Board Members
Make a commitment or exit gracefully

It's not uncommon for boards to spend six months discussing the roles, responsibilities, job description, and accountability of a prospective chief executive, and another six months going through the hiring process.

The irony is many of these boards have no formal roles, responsibilities, job descriptions, or systems of accountability for themselves. Their vetting process for board membership entails little more than spending an hour with a nominee over a cup of coffee.

This is dangerous. The roles and responsibilities of every board member—and the board itself—are every bit as important as those of the chief executive, and in some cases, more so.

Unfortunately, not enough board members believe this. They take their roles lightly because they feel it's the responsibility of the staff to do the work of the nonprofit since they're paid to do it. Many board members feel board membership is a "volunteer" position and whatever time, talent, and resources they provide is good enough. Participation is optional. Accountability is out of the question.

True, board members are volunteers. Men and women of the armed forces are, in some respects, volunteers too, and they go to war when told to do so. It's their role. It's the responsibility they signed up to perform. Just because board members are volunteers doesn't mean they get a pass from responsibilities and accountability. By accepting nomination to a board, members are accepting the battle cry to do the necessary work it takes to sustain their nonprofit and fulfill its mission.

One of the first things you should do with your founding board members is to establish a "roles and responsibilities" document for board members. I strongly suggest doing this before you submit your articles of incorporation, bylaws, or begin your 501c3 application. Make sure it addresses issues of accountability, performance evaluation, and specific duties board members are expected to perform. I have a comprehensive roles and responsibilities template you can have at a price that will fit your budget—Free! Just email tomiselin@gmail.com and ask for it.

The founding board members must be willing to adopt and abide by the roles and responsibilities of board membership before they bring on new board members. If they are unwilling to do this, you'll be launching your nonprofit with a bag of worms you'll one day regret holding. Set precedence from day one.

As you fold in new board members, they should fully understand their roles and responsibilities *before* they accept an offer to join. Require all board members to sign the roles and responsibilities document, and the entire board should review and sign the document once a year to renew their commitments and obligations.

Boards of more mature nonprofits should go one step further. They should create job descriptions for the board chair, president, vice president, secretary, treasurer, and any other officer positions. This helps the board and chief executive know who is responsible for what and who is accountable to whom. For example, if the secretary suddenly leaves, how can the board reasonably expect to fill the position if no one knows what the responsibilities include?

Too often boards want to avoid creating job descriptions and signing roles and responsibilities documents. They refuse to be managed or be held accountable. Make sure your board members understand board membership is not a weekend hobby or a position of entitlement; it's a serious responsibility and with it comes work and accountability.

If board members—potential or current—are unwilling to accept these terms, they shouldn't join the board, or migrate to a non-voting position such as an advisory board member or volunteer, or resign gracefully.

Provide oversight and develop policies

While it's not the job of the board to manage the operations of the organization, it is the board's responsibility to see to it the chief executive manages the financial and operational resources of the organization efficiently, effectively, and honestly.

The best way for the board to do this is through policy. Policies outline specific sets of rules, guidelines, and procedures by which the board and chief executive govern and manage various aspects of the board, staff, operations, and programming, all in an effort to hold the organization accountable to the broader community.

At a minimum, the organization should have a conflict of interest policy, confidentiality policy, and policies governing what the board and chief executive can and cannot do. Other common policies include a whistle-blower policy, a gift acceptance policy, and a retention and destruction policy. The chief executive will often draft policies requiring board approval for such things as firing employees, employee handbooks, and risk management.

The board should develop policies with the help of the chief executive, since the chief executive is often the person most knowledgeable about policy development and implementation.

The board is responsible for hiring, firing, and overseeing the chief executive. This means making sure the chief executive is fulfilling her roles and responsibilities outlined in her job description, acting fiscally responsible, fulfilling the objectives set forth in the strategic plan, and achieving the performance goals established in her annual evaluation.

Overseeing the work of the chief executive does not include meddling in daily operations or programming. For example, let's say a chief executive wants to hire two more programming staff. Her board should take a *strategic* perspective and ask her *why* she feels programming needs two new staff and how she and the organization plan to financially sustain the positions.

Board members should not write job descriptions for employees, take part in the interviewing process, or determine where the new staff should sit in the office. Board members need to clearly understand when they're sticking their oversight noses too far into the responsibilities of their chief executive and into the daily operations of their nonprofit.

Build and manage the board

The term used to describe the process of expanding and managing the board is called *board development*. It's a task that usually finds its way to the bottom of the board's ToDo list, but it's the job of the board chair to make sure it finds its way to the top. A good board member can take more than a year to find, so it's important your board make it an ongoing priority to cultivate a list of potential board members.

Remember, you must nominate board members who are authentically passionate about your organization's mission, fit into the culture of your board, provide legitimacy, and are willing to sink their teeth into the work needed to be done to fulfill your mission. No freeloaders. No sloths.

Potential board members need to know from the moment they talk to one of your board members that joining your board is not a club membership they've earned because of their business success, social status, or inherited name. They need to clearly understand board membership means responsibility, work, ownership, and accountability.

If potential board members are unwilling to accept this, then they shouldn't join your board—and you shouldn't encourage them to join. I cannot emphasize this point strongly enough: you must, absolutely must, do everything possible to ensure you elect high quality board members.

If you don't, you'll end up with a bunch of entitled cronies on your board and get nothing accomplished. Worse yet, you'll be stuck with them for the term of their membership and maybe longer—years longer!

Whatever the size of your nonprofit, you don't want to find yourself in this predicament. Be cautious. Be protective. Set term limits to three years or less. After a three-year term, require board members to undergo a thorough evaluation that includes feedback from the board, chief executive, and a handful of key staff. Keep evaluation responses anonymous. After a second or third term, establish a policy that requires board members to resign from the board for at least one year.

Let me quickly interject and say I do believe friends and business partners can make terrific board members. However, if you invite friends to join your board, first make sure that they are sincerely willing to work hard, make sacrifices, and contribute resources to make your nonprofit a success. Otherwise, you're likely to end up with a stale and combative board, and you may lose some friends in the process.

To ensure your board has the vibrant and committed members it needs to be productive and fulfill your mission, establish a tactical plan for board development. This should include a process for identifying, cultivating, recruiting, orienting, engaging, educating, inspiring, evaluating, rotating, and celebrating board members. It's a big task, but it will prove to be one of the most important you undertake. There are plenty of sources on the Web to help you develop such a plan.

Oversee legal and ethical issues and policies
Board membership is a serious responsibility. A judge won't buy the pity card your board chair offers after one of your participants becomes par-

alyzed in a car accident thanks to your volunteer bus driver who was drunk while driving your Special Olympics team home from a swimming event.

"But your honor, this is his first 'driving under the influence' violation and he has no speeding tickets. We're just a little nonprofit doing good work for children with disabilities. We can't afford the bad publicity or the money to fight a lawsuit."

Fat chance! In fact, if the court determines the cause of the injury was the result of gross negligence, your board may be *personally* liable for the legal fees required to fight the case and for any punitive damages awarded to the family. This means board members could lose some big money in the process. Really.

Boards can protect themselves to some extent by purchasing Directors and Officers insurance (if you don't have it, get it immediately.) This is a special type of liability insurance that protects board members from lawsuits when incidents like the one above happen.

However, if a judge determines an accident was an act of gross negligence, your board, not the staff or volunteers, could still be liable for fines and punitive damages even if you carry Directors and Officers insurance. For example, if the board chair knew the volunteer driver was drunk, but let him drive the bus anyway, a judge would probably categorize the board chair's action as gross negligence and the board chair could be held personally liable for damages.

Review important policies at least every two years
Boards have legal, ethical, and moral responsibilities to beneficiaries, constituents, and the community. The IRS and each state have laws outlining the legal responsibilities nonprofits must uphold. It's your board's responsibility to understand them, apply them, and monitor them.

When was the last time your board read and discussed your articles of incorporation and bylaws? Don't feel too embarrassed. I regularly talk with nonprofits that can't even find these documents and haven't a clue what they represent.

In case you don't already know, these documents provide the legal and operational framework for your nonprofit. Articles of incorporation define why you exist and your purpose to operate. Bylaws outline the structure, rules, and protocols of your board and your nonprofit.

Your board should review these documents, along with every one of your major policies every two years to ensure they are up-to-date and accurately reflect changes in nonprofit law and changes at your nonprofit.

The board also has the responsibility of making sure your nonprofit operates ethically. Are you following labor laws? Do you have policies covering bookkeeping and spending practices? Are there any business dealings with board members that might be considered a conflict of interest? If staff feel discriminated against, is there a process for them to safely talk about it? Has your state enacted any new nonprofit laws?

Ethics is a broad subject, but your board needs to ensure your nonprofit is operating on a platform of good morals and values defined by standards of excellence and sound policy.

Board membership might be a volunteer role, but just one serious incident of gross negligence and your board members could wind up giving more than just their time to your nonprofit; they may wind up giving away a chunk of their savings to settle a wrongful death lawsuit.

Help raise money and ensure fiscal responsibility

It's a primary responsibility of all board members to ensure financial resources are available to execute and sustain their nonprofit. This is not only a nonprofit best practice, but the IRS requires all nonprofits to understand this responsibility before they will issue 501c3 exempt status to nonprofit applicants.

Before any board member nominees join your board, it's imperative they *clearly* understand their responsibility to help raise money. No exceptions. Board members can formalize their fundraising commitments in writing by signing a copy of your nonprofit's roles and responsibilities policy outlining a board member's responsibility and commitment to raising money.

Still, no matter what policies are in place, or what documents are signed, board members are notorious for dodging fundraising responsibilities. If board members are short on time or shy about asking for money, it's important they know there are other ways they can help raise money.

They can provide lists of prospects, make introductions, cultivate relationships, host a dinner party, or help organize a fundraiser. Even mundane tasks such as writing thank-you letters are helpful.

You should also establish a policy requiring every board member to make an annual financial contribution. This is a standard best practice and don't let any board member convince you otherwise. Many foundations will not award grants unless every board member has made a contribution, and some foundations look to see what percentage of a nonprofit's annual income comes from its board members.

What message are you sending donors if you have board members unwilling to contribute themselves? Why should donors contribute if the board doesn't? What does it say about your nonprofit and your board members if the income of your nonprofit is $1 million, but less than $5,000 comes from your entire board, four of whom each have a net worth greater than $5 million?

It's imperative your board and each board member share the responsibility for the fundraising efforts of your nonprofit. Even if your chief executive or volunteer development officer is a gifted fundraiser, every board should establish annual fundraising goals for itself and all board members should make a commitment, in writing, how they plan to contribute to the fundraising efforts of the organization.

Fiscal responsibility for boards goes far beyond raising money, making contributions, and building reserve funds. Your board needs to take responsibility to oversee everything that involves money. This includes investments, real estate, bank accounts, financial statements, audits, IRS reporting, bookkeeping systems, and check writing, to name a few.

It's the responsibility and duty of your board to see to it these functions, and the policies and protocols governing them, are in place and managed responsibly. If your board has enough members, it should establish a finance committee to handle the financial responsibilities of the board.

Fundraising and financial oversight should not be left to the chief executive or a development officer. It's a key responsibility of *every* board member. What good is it if you have the world's most effective programming and the world's most efficient operations, but you have a set of board members unwilling to help raise money to support the people and hard work that created both? It's no good, that's what it is.

Set a clear precedent from day one; if board members are unwilling to raise money, contribute money, and be held accountable for the financial responsibilities of the organization, don't elect them to the board, or ask them to resign from the board. Addressing these issues may cause strife, but you must draw a line in the sand. Remain steadfast and do what is right, not what's convenient.

Keep an eye on the bigger picture

It's common for boards to get so caught up in the details of running a board that they lose sight of the bigger picture. Board meetings get bogged down with long-winded committee updates, decisions about the best caterer to use for an upcoming gala, and time spent reviewing architectural renderings of the staff's new office. These topics may be relevant and important, but boards also need to spend time discussing big picture items such as governance and strategy.

At your next board meeting, budget time for board members to reflect on the bigger picture. Ask them to look above the ground fog and scan the horizon. What do they see? What's on their minds?

You can facilitate big picture discussion by choosing to talk about topics such as strategic planning, long-term funding, changes in the economy, industry trends, upcoming legislation, brand image, program additions, operational efficiencies, roles and responsibilities, or staff morale.

Your board is the guardian of your mission. It's the board's responsibility to ensure that the decisions and direction of your nonprofit are in line with its mission and values. To do this well, boards need to set aside time on a regular basis to reflect on and discuss the big picture issues at hand.

Hire, evaluate, and fire the chief executive
Hiring
Your board has the critical role of hiring a chief executive. A wise choice can catapult your nonprofit to new heights; a poor choice can send you into a tailspin of disaster. In the last chapter, I covered the *type* of chief executive a nonprofit should hire or develop. Here, I'm going to focus on the *process* of hiring, evaluating, and firing a chief executive.

As I said, unmet expectations are the root of many conflicts between the board and chief executive. To reduce this risk, your board should write a comprehensive job description, compensation plan, and benefits package before it posts a job listing.

The job description should include roles and responsibilities, time off, board expectations, and performance measures. It should also include a brief overview of the management style and character traits you're looking for in a chief executive and the type of culture you've developed at your nonprofit.

During the interview process, the board must be honest and fully transparent about the state of the organization. Chief executives need to understand the history of an organization—good and bad. They need to hear about any board drama, disgruntled staff, inappropriate financial dealings, and sour business partnerships. The board should also ask the prospective executive about what expectations she has of the board, the staff, and the job.

Holding a phone interview and sharing a coffee at Starbucks is not an effective process for hiring a chief executive. Neither is having a four-hour grill session in front of a handful of board members. The best way to hire a chief executive is to observe one in action.

Once you've narrowed the field of candidates down to the top three, pay for them to visit your nonprofit for two or three days. During their stays, create various scenarios where candidates have to perform snippets of their job responsibilities so the board and staff can interact with them and observe how they function in real life situations.

Have them make presentations to the board, review financial statements with your accountant, participate in your programming as a volunteer, give a motivational talk at a staff meeting, and make a mock donor presentation to your fundraising team. Do not allow board members to sit in on the staff related interactions with the candidate, and make sure you design thorough and fair methods to evaluate performance.

I use various forms of this interviewing process when hiring executives and managers because it immediately exposes a candidate's strengths, weaknesses, and character traits. Seeing a candidate in action quickly reveals a person's true nature in ways a resumé or coffee interview cannot. This is my favorite technique for screening managers at all levels within an organization, and once you try it you'll know why.

After you've chosen a chief executive, make sure the board includes a probationary clause in the offer letter. Require that the chief executive undergo a performance review after 90 days, and only after a successful evaluation should the board vote to officially hire the chief executive. This may seem overly cautious, but the board should have an early dismissal plan in case the chief executive is a washout.

Evaluating

After the board hires a chief executive, it's the responsibility of the board to evaluate the performance of the chief executive each year. You should know, the IRS 990 form now asks whether or not a board annually evaluates its chief executive.

Boards will do themselves and their chief executive a great service by basing evaluations on specific, predetermined, measurable objectives and outcomes based on the nonprofit's strategic plan and the chief executive's job description.

Boards should be careful to avoid evaluating performance based on vague statements such as, "Did the executive do a good job of raising money?" or "How well did the executive get along with staff?" Questions such as these are unfair because they leave room for subjectivity and bias.

For example, if your strategic plan states your chief executive will be responsible to raise $200,000 a year, then it would be fair to ask whether she achieved her fundraising goal. How long did it take? What methods did she employ? How much money did she spend to achieve the goal? These are clear, measurable, and objective questions based on an established performance objective.

Soon after the evaluation process, the board, in collaboration with the chief executive, should establish goals, objectives, expectations, and performance measures for the upcoming year. If the board includes the chief executive in the evaluation process, she will be more motivated to achieve the outcomes expected of her.

Firing

Firing a chief executive, or forcing a resignation, is the responsibility of a board and is never easy. Even if the chief executive was a tyrant, you want the exit to be quiet and smooth. You need to protect your brand,

and it may be worth it to suck up a little and appease the chief executive by paying unused vacation days, presenting an appreciation award, hosting a farewell party, paying a bonus, or acknowledging her service publicly in some positive manner.

It's important the board work to flank any potential criticisms and negative repercussions that may come about as a result of firing a chief executive. The board should prepare a talking points document about the executive's departure so all board members speak in a single voice when talking about the matter publicly. Sharing this statement with the staff is also a good idea. One board member, preferably the board chair, should be the point of contact for all media.

If the relationship with the chief executive was contentious, I suggest the board member with the healthiest relationship with the chief executive take responsibility for all future communication with her.

Sometimes the unexpected happens. A chief executive may suddenly discover she is pregnant and decide to resign. An aging executive may have a heart attack and be forced to resign, and a young executive may suddenly leave to accept a higher paying job at a more prestigious nonprofit out of town.

Situations like these can cause chaos if a nonprofit is unprepared. Who is going to manage staff? Who will take over the executive's fundraising responsibilities? What happens if she walks out with her laptop? Who will talk with the media and handle damage control?

It's the board's responsibility to establish a plan and set policy to address all types of scenarios that may unfold if a chief executive's employment terminates. Carve out time with your board to talk about "what if" scenarios and, at a minimum, come up with at least a bullet-pointed outline of how the board would handle each situation.

You definitely want to establish emergency transition and succession plans in case your chief executive has an extended absence or suddenly departs.

Remember, the average length of a chief executive's employment is five years. Your board needs to plan—and expect—this type of turnover. Be wise; establish emergency plans early in your lifecycle so you can glide through the chaos when the unexpected happens.

Support the chief executive

If a board hires a great chief executive, it needs to trust its decision and support the executive to do her job without micromanaging her. If a board can't stay out of the way, the board or a few policies might need an overhaul. The responsibility of a board, as you recall, is to oversee operations, not meddle in them.

Peter Drucker, the famous nonprofit management consultant, had these words to say about board meddling: "A board that understands its real obligations and sets goals for its own performance won't meddle. But if you leave the board's role open and undefined, you'll get one that interferes with details and yet doesn't do its own job." Wise words.

A board should also support its chief executive by providing her with the training and mentoring she may need to efficiently and effectively manage the nonprofit. And if the board wants its chief executive to work hard, be happy, and stick around, it will also want to support opportunities that inspire its executive to pursue her personal aspirations.

Chief executives do thousands of hours of thankless tasks. They work late nights, weekends, and holidays in a tireless effort to manage all aspects of operations, programming, and fundraising. Two-thirds of chief executives leave their jobs because they feel unhappy or unappreciated—not because of lack of pay.

How happy is your chief executive? What is your board doing to encourage her? What has your board done to show her how much it appreciates her work and dedication? What is your board doing to support her personal and professional aspirations?

Start with a small board

The discussion above, though 16 pages in length, covers only a handful of the roles and responsibilities expected of chief executives and board members. There are many more, and you'd be wise to seek out credible resources to learn about others.

Now, let's continue with the subject of executive-board relationships. If you're thinking about starting a nonprofit, I suggest starting with a small number of board members. With fewer initial board members, it's easier to arrange schedules, make decisions, and develop a healthy executive-board relationship. I find small, nimble boards are more diligent about getting work done and have more fun in the process.

The smaller the board, the more critical it is that all board members, including the chief executive, be fully committed to fulfilling their roles and responsibilities. Set the bar high and remain steadfast.

Most states require a nonprofit to have at least three board members to incorporate. This is a good starting number. I strongly recommend you not launch a nonprofit with more than five board members. If you find you need more help at the board level during your startup stages, ask people to volunteer as committee members, or create an advisory board. To prevent your board from growing too quickly, establish guidelines in your bylaws that address board size and the pace of board growth.

If your nonprofit is more mature and you feel you have too many board members for the size of nonprofit you're running, lobby to change your bylaws to reduce term limits and set a maximum size for the number of board members. This will be a challenge, but you can reduce the skirmish by offering incentives to rotate members off the board into other areas of responsibility such as committees and advisory positions.

Encourage open and frequent communication
One of the best ways to nurture a healthy and productive executive-board relationship is through open, honest, and frequent communication. It all starts at the top. If communication between the chief executive and board chair is good, there is a high probability the communication between the chief executive and the entire board will be good.

The chief executive and board chair should have regular, in-person meetings to discuss operations and any major issues facing the board. They should also meet, or at least talk, before every board meeting to review the agenda items and important topics. Nothing is more reassuring to board members and staff than feeling the board chair and chief executive are getting along well and speaking in a unified voice.

Suggest that your board chair and chief executive sit next to each other at board meetings and that they run them in a collegial manner. Board meetings should encourage mutual compassion, constructive discussion, and respectful listening. The board chair and chief executive should always be willing to make time to talk with board members and help them become the best board members they can be.

Some people have very powerful personalities. They can dominate a conversation or steamroll another person's input. It's the responsibility of the chief executive and board chair to regulate the ebb and flow of conversation at board meetings and give everyone a chance to safely and openly share their thoughts and feelings.

You'd think the nonprofit world would attract caring and sensitive people, but it's common for board discussions and interactions to get personal, sometimes vile. If a personality conflict pops up, it's the responsibility of the board chair to handle it immediately. If the board chair is involved, the entire board may need to get involved.

Everyone is too busy to deal with board drama and your nonprofit is too busy to let it fester. In some cases, it's best to have a respected honorary board member or consultant mediate the conflict in an effort to resolve problems between the chief executive and the board, or between board members.

To ward off petty fights and bickering, establish—and enforce—a three strike policy for derogatory comments, vindictive emails, gossip, and negative attitudes. That's right, negative attitudes. A board should not tolerate members who are too immature to act in a professional manner.

Violators should receive verbal and written warnings from the board chair for the first two strikes, and the third strike should result in removal from the board. No exceptions. In the case of the chief executive, a third strike should result in dismissal.

Board members should know from the first day you ask them to join your board that your board is running a tight ship. Yes, you have fun, work hard, and exercise compassion, but you will not tolerate behavior that hurts people or hampers the mission. Board members must understand they are responsible for being thoughtful and engaged leaders, not passive stewards.

Have fun outside the boardroom

Another way to deepen executive-board relations is to spend time together outside the boardroom in fun, relaxed settings. The setting can be as simple as a wine and cheese party at someone's home, a barbeque at a park, or an outdoor jazz concert. The duration of the event is not important; what's important is that everyone takes time to get to know one another outside boardroom walls.

It's also important the chief executive make an effort to spend one-on-one time with each board member throughout the year. This is much easier when a nonprofit has only a handful of board members, but it's still feasible even if a board has 10 or 12 members. Meeting just once every six months for a cup of coffee, glass of wine, or a short walk can do wonders to nurture a relationship.

Roundtable discussions
Another way to improve executive-board relations is for the chief executive to host monthly "roundtable discussions." These discussions are informal board member gatherings in casual, social environments. It could be a simple breakfast in the morning, a casual picnic or lunch, or sharing a glass of wine during happy hour at a wine bar. Attendance is not required.

The purpose of the roundtable discussions is to provide board members an opportunity to hang out with the chief executive in a casual group setting on a regular basis and get to know one another. It's also a time to ask questions, discuss topics, and brainstorm ideas without an agenda, time constraints, or fear of embarrassment.

If your chief executive holds roundtable discussions, encourage her to invite one or two key staff each time. This will provide board members a chance to learn more about programming and operations, and it also provides the staff an opportunity to get to know board members on a personal level.

Board meeting dinners
One of the best ways to combine the casual atmosphere of a roundtable discussion and the seriousness of a boardroom setting is to hold your board meetings over dinner. Potluck style dinners work best to reduce the burden on the host. Start the evening with beverages and a few light appetizers. This allows everyone a chance to unwind from the day and catch up on the latest happenings in each other's personal lives.

When dinner starts, the board chair or chief executive should facilitate dinner conversation by encouraging attendees to share personal stories for 30 minutes before diving into the board agenda. Starting slowly and keeping things personal will establish a lighthearted, friendly tone for a productive evening.

I suggest hosting a board meeting dinner at least quarterly. If your board is small enough and you have two or three passionate cooks on your board, you may consider hosting all your board meetings over dinner. With delicious food, great wine, and nice people, I can guarantee your board will look forward to board meetings. As a result, the board will develop close friendships and a deep sense of respect and admiration for one another, all while working as a team to propel the mission.

As an alternative to dinner, start your boardroom meetings 30 minutes early and offer beverages and appetizers. This will at least provide time for mingling and personal chit-chat. No matter what you choose to do, your chief executive and board members should make a commitment to get out of the boardroom regularly to deepen their relationships, share some laughs, and have some fun.

Takeaways

The most successful nonprofits are those with passionate chief executives and board members who work well together, understand and fulfill their responsibilities, and have fun in the process.

Nonprofits that trivialize the importance of board-executive relations inevitably find themselves in a ring of drama and conflict. Too stubborn and prideful to solve their relationship issues, they face off like pit bulls and claw and bite each other to the death—death of the nonprofit, that is.

Do not tolerate corrosive relationships. They will eat at the soul of your nonprofit like acid. If you sense a corrosive relationship unfolding, address the problem immediately and take measures to prevent the problem from recurring, even if it means removing a board member or firing the chief executive. You must have zero tolerance for corrosive behavior. Zero.

The first thing you must do to develop healthy executive-board relations is to make it a top priority. Board members need to create documents outlining the philosophy and policies governing the executive-board relationship. Whatever philosophy they adopt, it should include the concepts of collegiality, equality, respect, and good communication.

Healthy executive-board relations also require everyone to work *together* to fulfill the mission. To accomplish this, you'll need to develop a specific set of clearly defined roles, responsibilities, and job descriptions for the chief executive and board members, especially the officers.

You will also need to set up various structures and procedures to hold people accountable to fulfill their responsibilities and make good on the work they committed to perform.

Many board tasks and chief executive tasks will be distinctly different, but collectively everyone's work should harmonize. Again, make it a priority to do these things as early in your lifecycle as possible. The sooner they're in place, the better chance you'll have to succeed and the better chance you'll have to avoid costly mistakes that can haunt you for years.

When humility, selflessness, kindness, helpfulness, gratitude, and servant leadership become words used to define the relationship between your chief executive and board, you'll know the relationship is strong, healthy, and productive. It will be music to your ears when you feel each is asking, "What can be done to help the other?" not "What can the other do for me?"

Finally, one of the most undervalued attributes of a healthy executive-board relationship is a vibrant *friendship* between the two. An acquaintance based relationship will work, but a professional, friendship based relationship will thrive.

We all know the best way to build a strong friendship is to spend time together. Create opportunities for your chief executive and board members to spend time together outside the confines of the boardroom in casual, social settings to deepen their relationships and share some laughs.

If you're running a gold standard nonprofit, everyone will be selflessly busting their butts to make a difference. Along the way, make sure everyone is taking time to smell the roses. Host dinner parties, go hiking, tell jokes, and find ways to celebrate your achievements and milestones on a regular basis. You deserve it!

CHAPTER 8

Engaged Volunteers
Turning passion into productivity

Volunteers are the unsung heroes and heroines of the nonprofit world. They provide immeasurable value and contribution with little expectation of praise or recognition.

It's surprising how few nonprofits take advantage of the power and value of volunteers. They either have no volunteer program, or they have a program that does a great job of soliciting volunteers, but a poor job of engaging and retaining them.

The result in either case is a tremendous loss of opportunity, value, and money, and the disappointment of many people who had high hopes of making a difference in a mission they believed in.

Why are engaged volunteers important?

Having engaged volunteers is a *First Things First* principle because developing a group of skilled, committed, and engaged volunteers is the single most effective thing a nonprofit can do to leverage its human capital to fulfill its mission at minimal cost.

Volunteers are nonprofit gold. They provide much more value to a nonprofit than lending a helping hand on a Saturday morning to fill food boxes to feed hungry families. Volunteers also provide skilled labor and expertise. They are advocates to spread the good news about noble missions. They are donors willing to write checks. They are conduits to influential people and businesses, and they supply intangibles such as love, hope, passion, compassion, generosity, and gratitude. Even children and teenage volunteers provide significant contributions.

The value of quality volunteers is evident. The challenge is creating an effective volunteer program that turns interested volunteers into long-term committed volunteers actively engaged in helping your nonprofit fulfill its mission. This is a big task, and to be successful requires a substantial investment in time, money, talent, and effort.

Most importantly, if you have hopes of expanding your programming and services, you'll want to launch a volunteer program as early in your lifecycle as possible. This is critical because you'll need to leverage every ounce of human capital to handle the workload as you begin to expand and grow.

You'll also want to build a volunteer program early on because if you're forced to start a volunteer program in the middle of a major expansion phase, you're sure to disrupt your momentum. Do the right thing, right from the start: launch a volunteer program as soon as you start soliciting volunteers. First things first!

Case Study: Now, that's volunteer value!

Two weeks into the restructuring efforts of Sun Valley Adaptive Sports, I asked the program director to provide me a list of our volunteers. The list had 10 names. I asked how many were committed enough to show up on a moment's notice if we had an immediate need. She shrugged, looked down at the floor and whispered, "Two."

I remember thinking, "Two! . . . What a small number of volunteers for a six-year-old nonprofit with so much labor-intensive programming." To acknowledge our small base of volunteers and get them fired up about our upcoming plans, we arranged a volunteer appreciation party. We sent handwritten invitations stating the party would include appetizers, wine, and gifts of appreciation. To our disappointment, only two volunteers showed; the two the director expected to show.

The low turnout wasn't really a surprise because SVAS had no volunteer program. No one was assigned to solicit, train, engage, and thank volunteers. In many ways, volunteers were treated as "helpers" called upon in "need only" situations.

It also didn't help that the founder, who had since left SVAS, felt volunteers were a liability to the SVAS adaptive ski program and should not be allowed to help, unless they had a "professional" certification. This was not an industry practice. At the time, more than 90 percent of adaptive ski programs in the nation had volunteer based programs and almost half of these programs were 100 percent volunteer operated.

We knew there were dozens of potential volunteers in the community willing to help SVAS and we knew we couldn't expand our programming without a strong volunteer base. So, without delay, we launched a volunteer program, modeling it after the most respected adaptive sports volunteer programs in the nation.

Our first order of business was hiring a full-time volunteer coordinator. We decided on a full-time position instead of a part-time one because we had big plans to quickly expand our programming to serve dozens of people with disabilities locally and regionally, and hundreds of wounded veterans from around the country who were returning from Iraq and Afghanistan.

The volunteer coordinator jumpstarted the program by writing a strategic plan that outlined how she planned to build and manage the program. She created a handbook outlining the roles, responsibilities, and expectations of volunteers. She wrote dozens of checklists and training manuals. She also designed a custom database to manage names, created a blog to keep existing volunteers informed, and set up outreach events to solicit and train new volunteers.

Her goal was to train volunteers so well, and engage them so frequently, that they would be skilled enough to help our participants with the same proficiency as our staff therapists.

It worked. After two years of soliciting, training, engaging, and acknowledging, our volunteer base grew to 150. After four years, it had grown to 325. Of course, not all our volunteers fell into the category of "committed and fully engaged," but more than half were. Of the remaining 50 percent, I'd say 25 percent helped occasionally, 20 percent helped irregularly, and 5 percent helped only once or twice a year.

The volunteer program was wildly successful. It took a ton of work by an extremely bright and very dedicated coordinator. In the end, the thousands and thousands of volunteer hours allowed SVAS to grow its programming at a rate of 100 percent a year, double what we expected. It also allowed SVAS to improve the therapeutic quality of its programming because so many volunteers had become highly trained as adaptive instructors and therapist assistants.

Had we paid trained staff to do the same work as our volunteers, it would have cost SVAS more than $500,000 a year in labor costs. In 2007, this would have been 40 percent of our budget.

It's important to note our volunteers provided much more than a few hours of work here and there. They provided many skills we needed and lacked funds to pay for. Financial planners gave us free investment advice. Physical therapists offered our wounded veterans free services. Accountants completed our IRS reporting documents at no charge, and CEOs introduced us to corporate foundation executives. These "in-kind" contributions, and many others, totaled more than $200,000 in 2007. Now, that's volunteer value!

SVAS did a lot of wise things at the right time to become a gold stand-ard nonprofit of national prominence so quickly. Looking back, I would have to say one of the biggest contributing factors to our rapid growth and success was our amazing volunteer program. We were also fortunate to have a remarkable volunteer coordinator who worked efficiently and tirelessly to engage hundreds of volunteers that were passionate about making a significant impact in the lives of people with disabilities.

The result *was* significant. Our volunteers helped SVAS transform an entire industry and, in the process, made lasting and meaningful change in the lives of thousands of people with disabilities.

If you have big dreams or want to accomplish the impossible, you're going to need help—lots of it. The smartest thing you can do to get the help you need at a cost you can afford is to build a quality volunteer program as early in your lifecycle as possible.

Tactics and Tips
Hire or appoint a volunteer coordinator
If you're going to start a volunteer program, you'll need someone to manage it. If you have less than 50 volunteers, offer the position of volunteer coordinator to one or two board members or a couple of vol-unteers. It's a good task for engaging board members because the job is very hands-on and board members will learn a lot about the operational aspects of your programs and the effort required to run them.

You could assign a staff person to the job, but if you're like most nonprofits, labor resources are in short supply. The best way to involve staff at this level is to have one of your staff oversee the position and the associated job responsibilities. This way they can focus the bulk of their time on programming and operations where their expertise is needed most.

If your nonprofit has 51 to 100 volunteers, and you can afford it, I suggest hiring a volunteer coordinator, even if only on a part-time basis. With 101-150 volunteers, I strongly suggest hiring a part-time or full-time coordinator because there are too many volunteers to manage and too many tasks to juggle not to have someone solely dedicated to managing the work.

You may think a couple of board members or volunteers can handle the workload of managing 120 volunteers on a part-time basis, but I can tell you from experience, it's simply too much work, especially if your programming requires a substantial amount of training and communication.

Burnout is also common. The last headache you need in the middle of a growth spurt is a part-time volunteer coordinator who walks in the office one morning and says, "I'm burned out. I don't want to be volunteer coordinator any longer; I just want to volunteer." The risk of this happening will be much less if the position is a paid one.

If you have more than 150 volunteers, you should definitely hire a full-time coordinator. At this level, the role of a volunteer coordinator becomes a serious managerial position, requiring full-time attention. Without a full-time coordinator to solicit, train, engage, manage, and thank 150, 200, or 300 volunteers, a volunteer program will eventually trip and stumble, resulting in dozens of underused, unhappy volunteers.

When you're a very small nonprofit, it's enough to assign the position of volunteer coordinator to willing board members and volunteers. As you grow, especially if you grow quickly, it's essential you hire an experienced and skilled coordinator, because the better job you do to build a program of engaged volunteers, the more resources you'll have to fulfill your mission.

Hire a volunteer coordinator with the right skill set
The success of your volunteer program will depend largely on the type of person you appoint or hire to run the program. When filling the position, you'll want to be on the lookout for a number of specific work skills and personality traits.

Master organizer
The most important skill you'll want to look for when hiring a volunteer coordinator is the skill of organization. It's his job to match the needs of

your nonprofit with the time, skills, and talents of your volunteers. He oversees the process of soliciting, training, engaging, and thanking volunteers. He makes calls, sends emails, manages calendars, writes blogs, coordinates events, and does many of these tasks simultaneously, under pressure, and with limited resources. If you want all this done with ease and perfection, you must hire a master organizer.

Easy-going and friendly

The most important personality trait you want to look for is someone who is easy-going and friendly. Coordinators manage and talk with hundreds of people on a regular basis and it's their job to get people motivated and excited to volunteer.

If your coordinator is fun and friendly, and bubbles with enthusiasm, your volunteers are more likely to volunteer because people like to volunteer where they have a meaningful experience, make friends, and have a good time. The job is not for people with a low stress tolerance. Avoid hiring anyone who seems to be uptight, edgy, or has a history of being stressed out.

Superior writing and speaking skills

A volunteer coordinator should have superior writing and speaking skills. He writes hundreds of emails, makes thousands of phone calls, and gives dozens of presentations. You should hire someone with strong enough writing and speaking skills that you'd trust him to write an inspiring press release, make cold calls to strangers, and give motivating public speaking presentations.

Flexible and tolerant

A volunteer coordinator should also have a flexible and tolerant personality. This is an important trait because the position requires working with and managing people of varying ages, backgrounds, education, and experience. It takes a lot of patience and understanding to handle constant change and the personal drama that can unfold when interacting with people of different personalities and skill sets. Look for a coordinator who is open-minded and nonjudgmental.

Basic business skills

Other important skills include marketing, technology, and finance. A coordinator does not have to be an expert in these areas, but proficiency is very useful. Coordinators are typically responsible for designing flyers, updating databases, and creating budgets. The more efficiently and effectively a coordinator can perform such tasks, the more efficiently and effectively the program will run.

Entrepreneurialism
One last attribute worth mentioning is the spirit of entrepreneurialism. The best coordinators are motivating leaders who can think outside the box and take initiative. A coordinator's work is dynamic. Hire someone who embraces change and welcomes the unexpected.

Your volunteer coordinator is responsible for managing one of your most important assets: human capital. The more volunteers you engage, the more free labor and resources you'll have available to build a gold standard nonprofit and fulfill your mission. This is one of the most undervalued concepts in the nonprofit world. You'd be wise to reflect on the significance of this concept and put as much time into hiring a great volunteer coordinator as you would a great program director.

Establish a plan and create a budget
If you want a great volunteer program, you'll need to value it and invest in it. Your volunteer program should have a strategic plan and a budget. The plan should detail how the program intends to solicit, train, engage, and acknowledge volunteers. It should also include evaluation tools to measure volunteer effectiveness and track involvement.

Make sure you budget enough funds to adequately operate the program. You'll need to budget funds to hire a talented coordinator who has the skills to build and manage a great program. You will also want to budget funds for training, office supplies, posters, thank-you cards, parties, and other small tokens of appreciation.

Engaging volunteers means making volunteers *feel* engaged. Each dollar you spend on recognition and appreciation will come back many times over in the form of service and commitment.

Match skills with needs
One of the most important things you can do to engage volunteers is to make sure they are doing what they want to do. If someone signs on with the expectation of planting seedlings to rebuild a redwood forest and then you call her last minute to stuff envelopes for your annual fundraising mailer, there's a good chance you'll end up with a dissatisfied volunteer.

Sure, she may occasionally oblige a last minute administrative request, but if she continually finds herself in an office with a sore tongue more often than in a forest with sore hands, you run the risk of losing her as a volunteer.

To prevent this type of thing from happening, your coordinator should conduct a "skill and interest" assessment soon after a volunteer signs on. The goal is to discover and match the interests, passions, skills, and availability of a volunteer with the needs of your nonprofit. After reviewing the assessment, your coordinator will want to set up a meeting with the volunteer.

Meeting face-to-face gives a coordinator a chance to fine-tune the matching process, answer questions, review training requirements, discuss expectations, express gratitude, and get the volunteer excited about the impact her efforts will make. It's also a chance for a coordinator to learn more about the volunteer's character, personality, values, and interests.

The formula is simple: the more closely you match a volunteer's skills, interests, personality, and availability with the needs of your nonprofit, the more likely the volunteer will remain committed, happy, and engaged.

Establish a team leadership initiative
As your programs grow, so will your need for volunteers. If your volunteer base grows to 200 or more, it will be almost impossible for one coordinator to adequately manage this many people, especially if you have multiple programs serving different types of beneficiaries. One person can only do so much.

The solution is to encourage your volunteer coordinator to create a network of willing and capable volunteers he believes can lead and train other groups of volunteers to manage the key responsibilities and tasks of running programs and events.

At SVAS, we called this network our "Team Leader Initiative." It was basically a "train the trainer" model of training volunteers to help run our programs and events. The team leader model is an effective tactic to engage star volunteers because it gives them a deeper sense of program ownership and responsibility. It also frees the volunteer coordinator from many hands-on tasks so he can focus his efforts on the high-level needs of the volunteer program.

Provide frequent training and education

Volunteers know they are a form of unpaid labor, but they don't want to feel like they are. Training and education opportunities are excellent ways to build the culture of your volunteer base, engage them, and make them feel valued and appreciated.

Training is also good risk management. You certainly wouldn't want an untrained high school student assigned to a seven-year-old girl with a history of seizures. It's important that volunteers understand the inherent dangers of their work and it's your coordinator's job, and the responsibility of your nonprofit, to train and educate volunteers so they are qualified to do their jobs in a safe, professional manner. No one wants to see an injury or face a lawsuit.

In many cases, volunteers view ongoing training and education as a perk to working with a nonprofit because they get a chance to improve a particular skill set or learn something new. For example, SVAS, in conjunction with the Sun Valley Resort, paid to have certified clinicians from around the country visit Sun Valley to teach our ski instructors and volunteers the latest adaptive ski instruction techniques.

This was done at no cost to instructors or volunteers. The result was more qualified instructors for the resort and more engaged SVAS volunteers anxious to apply their newly acquired skills to a growing population of adaptive skiers.

The more SVAS found ways to help volunteers earn certification or continuing education credits as part of their training, the more eager they were to provide volunteer services for our programs. Think about ways you can train and educate your volunteers and provide added value to their volunteer experience.

When hosting volunteer training sessions, you'll want to make them simple, brief, meaningful, and fun. Schedule training sessions at times convenient to volunteers, not your staff.

This means you'll want to host training sessions in the evenings or on the weekends. It's important to keep volunteers informed with short emails, blog posts, or through social media, but be cautious about frequency; too much information will "tune out" and turn off volunteers.

You'll also want to take time during training sessions to share snippets of information about your nonprofit. Share the story of how your nonprofit started. Tell funny stories about volunteers. Inform them of the latest staff and programming changes. Share the board's vision and what the organization hopes to accomplish, and provide opportunities for volunteers to tour your office to meet staff and board members.

Regular training and education sessions keep volunteers engaged because it shows you care about them and are willing to invest time in them so they can serve the organization.

Require commitment

Many nonprofits shy away from asking volunteers to make time and work commitments. They believe volunteers are offering their time for free, so asking for commitments is an imposition on those generous enough to volunteer in the first place.

Actually, the opposite is true. Most volunteers prefer structured time commitments so they can manage their busy schedules. Think of your own schedule; it's a lot easier to schedule a business meeting or your daughter's soccer game if you know the time and place of the meeting or game ahead of time.

Though most volunteers will not admit it, they get annoyed when their favorite nonprofit calls late at night or last minute saying, "We're in a pinch, can you help collect tickets at tonight's program?" Or, "I'm sure you're busy this weekend, but we could really use your help to organize Saturday's fundraiser." Yes, emergencies do happen, but when poor planning and random, desperate calls become the norm, you can bet volunteers will start screening your calls.

It's not fair to expect volunteers to drop everything and come to your rescue, especially your teenage volunteers. Some people have difficulty saying no, and by saying yes, it may, unknowingly, put stress on a volunteer and her family. She may have to change a work schedule, arrange for daycare, or cancel a romantic night out.

Your coordinator and volunteer leaders need to be sensitive to the personal lives and busy schedules of volunteers when asking them to help. One of the simplest things you can do to engage volunteers and to make them feel you value their busy lives is to work with them to create a personalized volunteer commitment calendar. These commitments can be daily, weekly, monthly, by program, or by task. The goal is to get volunteers involved in a manner that fits their busy schedules and lifestyles.

With new volunteers, keep time commitments to a minimum. Give them plenty of opportunities to dip their toes in the volunteer water before asking them where they'd like to dive in. Make it easy for them to see and do a variety of tasks. Many times, volunteers say they want to help with administrative work, but as soon as they get a chance to help a young girl with spina bifida learn to swim, they realize they'd rather be in the scene than behind it.

Committed volunteers are engaged volunteers, so make it possible for volunteers to commit to regular participation in a capacity they can manage and a schedule that fits their lifestyle.

Give regular praise and recognition
No volunteer with a genuine heart for service is going to expect any type of praise or recognition for the time and effort they give. But I assure you, even the most humble and selfless volunteer feels warm and fuzzy when acknowledged for her work and dedication.

The praise and recognition you give doesn't have to be loud and public, but it should be frequent and sincere. A handwritten note, personal call, or brief one-on-one conversation acknowledging a volunteer's service and sacrifice can fuel a volunteer's passion for weeks.

If you want happy, committed, and engaged volunteers, make it a priority for your volunteer coordinator, volunteer leaders, key staff, and board members to express their gratitude to volunteers often, and with sincerity. Doing so will inspire volunteers to go the extra mile with a wide smile.

Provide benefits and perks
One way to recognize volunteers and keep them engaged is to provide meaningful benefits and perks. Perhaps one of your board members owns a theater and is willing to offer half-priced movie tickets to volunteers for every 10 hours of service they provide. Or, maybe you design a volunteer benefits program where volunteers earn points for hours of service, which can be redeemed for caps, T-shirts, coffee cards, access to concerts, or the use of sports equipment.

At SVAS, our big perk was offering lift tickets. For every five hours volunteers helped with our snowsports program, they earned a free lift ticket, good for a full day of skiing or snowboarding at the Sun Valley Resort. With tickets costing more than $80 a day, this was an extravagant perk for volunteers, some of whom could not otherwise afford to ski.

You don't have to offer perks as lavish as lift tickets to keep volunteers engaged, but whatever perks you offer, they should be meaningful and show volunteers how much you value their service.

Takeaways

Building a volunteer program with committed, skilled, and engaged volunteers is the most important thing you can do to leverage the human capital of your nonprofit. They provide skills and experience. They offer wisdom and influence. They promote your mission, they donate money, and they do it for free!

For you, however, there's a price to pay. It takes time, money, talent, and effort to build a great volunteer program. The job calls for a professional and requires a systematic plan to solicit, train, engage, motivate, manage, and recognize volunteers. And to get the most out of your volunteer program, you must value the program as highly as you value your most prized programs and services.

The greater your desire to expand your programs and services, the more important it is to establish a volunteer program early on in your lifecycle. Why? Because volunteers provide the human capital you need to grow and expand, but that you can't afford to hire.

Building a program early on will also allow you to sustain your expansion momentum when it happens, since you'll already have a program and volunteers in place, instead of stalling or derailing your expansion efforts because you were forced to divert time, money, and resources to start a program.

Individually and collectively, volunteers want to feel they are making a difference. They want to feel connected to something bigger than themselves. The more your volunteers feel their service provides value and the more they feel you value them—and *need* them—the more committed and engaged they will be.

You can show volunteers from age 8 to 80 that you value them by carefully matching their skills and interests with your needs, providing useful training and educational opportunities, asking for specific time commitments, and offering frequent praise and gratitude.

You can also show your volunteers you value them by offering meaningful perks and benefits to acknowledge their service and by establishing a leadership initiative to give star volunteers a greater stake in the noble work you're doing.

It's your responsibility to engage volunteers, fusing them to the soul of your mission and making them feel like precious gems in the process. If you do, they will prove to be your nonprofit's greatest treasure, providing vast amounts of social wealth in forms of time, money, skills, expertise, and influence as you build a gold standard nonprofit. If you don't, they will tune out and sign off, and offer their priceless time and resources to the nonprofit down the block.

CHAPTER 9

Praise and Gratitude

Saying thank you again and again

T he nonprofit world is a world of giving spirits, selfless motives, and compassionate hearts. People generously give their money, time, and expertise and expect little in return. So they say.

The truth is, though few will admit it, most donors, volunteers, staff, board members, and business partners like to feel appreciated and recognized for their contributions. It's not because of pride or ego. Rather, it's a deep sense of wanting to feel their contributions are valued and significant and, in some cases, a feeling *they* are valued and significant.

Why is praise and gratitude important?

Praise and gratitude is a *First Things First* principle because acknowledging people for their work and contributions is one of the easiest ways a nonprofit can deepen its culture and strengthen the commitment of those passionate to support and fulfill its mission.

By expressing praise and gratitude, you're investing in the human capital of your nonprofit. Again, this is an important concept to grasp because the more people you have willing to give their time, money, skills, and influence, the more resources you'll have to achieve your goals, fulfill your mission, and become a gold standard nonprofit.

I touched on the importance of praise and gratitude in varying degrees in previous chapters, but it deserves its own chapter because the principle is absolutely fundamental to the long-term success and sustainability of any nonprofit, yet it's grossly undervalued and often neglected.

In the last month, how many major donors have you taken out for coffee or lunch for no other reason than to thank them for their donation and to express the impact their donation made on a particular program? How many times have you thanked your business partners *in person* for their in-kind contributions? How would each of your staff rate your board's efforts to make them feel valued?

If you fail to express appreciation and gratitude for people's contributions, their enthusiasm and commitment will fade. Volunteers will leave, donors will stop giving, staff will become discouraged, and support from business partners will cease.

However, if you make a regular and sincere effort to show people you care about them and their contributions, they will repay your gratitude and appreciation with unwavering commitments and generous contributions that exceed expectations. First things first!

Case Study: Front-page gratitude

A reporter sympathetic to your cause is one of the most important allies you can have in your efforts to fulfill your mission. A front-page story in a local paper can motivate donors to give money and encourage volunteers to sign up. A feature article in a national magazine can catapult your brand, deepen your level of credibility, and inspire hundreds to write checks to support your cause.

Reporters are a tough bunch. They typically sit in cubicles most of the day with stacks of old newspapers and computer technology piled high around them. Advertising reps, production assistants, and editors scurry about. Their "war room" is noisy and disruptive and smells like copy toner and stale coffee. Deadlines loom and the buzz of stress is as loud as the cacophony of ringing phones.

The job of reporting is difficult and often lonely. This is why I made it a point to express my gratitude to reporters and editors for the articles and features they published about Sun Valley Adaptive Sports. At the very least, I'd send a thoughtful, *handwritten* card thanking them for their time and effort, and I would always include a few sentences telling them about the impact their article or blog had on SVAS.

I made a similar effort toward all types of media personnel. At least once every six months, I would meet with a variety of local and regional reporters, anchors, and producers to thank them, in person, for the work they did to cover our programs, especially the programming we were doing to rehabilitate veterans that had been severely wounded in Iraq and Afghanistan.

These meetings were brief, usually an hour or so over a cup of coffee. I made an effort to keep the conversation centered on their interests and work, not mine. If they did ask questions about SVAS, I'd spin my answer to include how much money we raised after their article about us ran in the paper, or how many volunteers we signed up.

When national media covered our programming, I was quick to contact the reporter or producer to let them know the response we received from Pentagon officials, members of Congress, or White House staff. They were always thankful for these types of calls because expressions of gratitude and appreciation to national media are rarer than you might imagine.

As you live in the nonprofit world, you realize reporters and producers have choices. How often they choose to cover the work you're doing will greatly depend on how well you treat them.

Sun Valley is a community of 25,000, yet there are more than 150 non-profits registered in the county. SVAS received nearly twice the print and television coverage of other nonprofits in the area. Why? Some would say we had timely and compelling stories to tell—helping children, teens, and adults with disabilities learn sports and recreational activities, and helping rehabilitate wounded veterans.

I agree, having compelling stories to tell backed by quality programming helped attract media, but I believe the frequency and quality of exposure we received had just as much to do with the relationships we established and nurtured with media representatives covering our stories as the stories themselves.

For example, instead of sending a press release to a random Associated Press email address in hopes of securing a feature, we'd send it directly to an AP reporter and follow up with a phone call. Once we had a reporter on the line, we'd tell him about one of our upcoming therapeutic sports camps we were hosting for wounded veterans and then invite him to participate in (not just observe) the camp.

This was a major differentiator between us and other nonprofits. I can't think of a single instance when a reporter turned down our offer to spend a day teaching a double-leg amputee how to alpine ski, or a blind veteran how to fly fish.

By immersing reporters into our programs as much as any volunteer, we enabled them to collect first-hand, compelling accounts of the innovative ways we were changing the lives of people participating in our programs.

Reporters ate it up. In fact, they regularly *called us* asking when they could participate again, and it was not uncommon for a reporter to become a SVAS volunteer after just one immersion experience.

In some respects, it seemed like the media was thanking us more than we were thanking them. We were giving them amazing personal stories that touched the souls of their readers and they thanked us by publishing one feature story after another.

No matter how frequent our coverage, we never took it for granted. Staff always sent some sort of thank-you card or token of appreciation, no matter the size or type of coverage we received. We also hosted media appreciation parties, sent handmade thank-you cards from kids in our programs, and sent endless amounts of SVAS hats and T-shirts.

I know the media appreciated our efforts because they'd send thank-you letters and emails in return saying how rare it was for them to receive sincere praise and gratitude for the work they did.

It's important to note, we didn't express praise and gratitude to the media because we thought we'd get special attention (okay, we did a little). Rather, we expressed our praise and gratitude because it was the right thing to do!

In the end, the time and effort we put forth to nurture our relationships with all types of media paid off—big time! The dozens of articles and hours of television coverage brought massive amounts of attention to our programming.

The widespread coverage provided credibility to our programming and mission, shaped public opinion, influenced legislation, transformed a local brand into a national brand, and led to millions in donations.

If you want similar results, start making friends with the media and express sincere praise and gratitude for the coverage they provide.

~ ~ ~

Tactics and Tips
Make praise and gratitude a priority
The principle of praise and gratitude extends far beyond thanking media for articles and features. It should be front and center in the minds of every staff, volunteer, and board member when interacting with anyone connected to your nonprofit. The best way to do this is to include the principle as one of the facets you define for your culture. This way, everyone will know you value the principle as much as any other cultural facet or core value.

You will also want to adopt this principle early on in your lifecycle. This is important because you often get only one chance to make a favorable impression of gratitude. For example, let's say you visit a local ski shop and ask them for a discount on rental equipment for the ski program you run for children with disabilities. If you come off as entitled, prideful, and unappreciative, the owner may help once but her door might be closed the next time you come knocking for a favor.

On the other hand, if your words and actions are positive, sincere, and grateful, the doors will probably swing wide open the next time you come knocking. Make a good first impression with memorable acts of praise and gratitude.

Keep it simple
Americans are notorious for being excessive. But when it comes to praise and gratitude, less is better. For example: "Thank you, Leslie, for taking time during your lunch hour to help me design this week's newspaper ad." "Steve, I want you to know how grateful I am to you for driving Edith to the senior center yesterday. She loved your jokes and told me it was the first time she'd laughed in months." "Pam, I want you to know how much I appreciate the extra hours you've been putting in lately; it means a lot to me and to the parents of this new program."

Simple expressions of praise and gratitude like these mean more to the recipient than you may expect. For some, even a genuine "Well done!" "Great job!" or "You're the best!" can inspire a program manager for weeks, give a board member a deeper sense of appreciation, and build the confidence of a young intern.

Expressions of praise and gratitude should come from everyone connected with the organization, not just the chief executive, board chair, and program director. The volunteer coordinator should have a system to thank and acknowledge volunteers. Managers should have a system to validate and praise staff, and the board should have a system to give thanks and show appreciation to major donors.

Whether it's a business partner, a new office manager, or a longtime donor, it's essential your nonprofit have systems in place to express its praise, gratitude, and appreciation to everyone committed to helping, no matter how small the contribution.

Do it often
You're busy. Your staff is busy. Your board is busy. Everyone's busy. Donors, volunteers, and others closely connected with your nonprofit know you're busy. So, when a staff or a board member carves out time to thank someone by making a call, writing a letter, or meeting for a glass of wine, it will make a substantial impact because people know your staff and board members have gone out of their way to make them feel special.

No matter how busy you think you are, or how often you think you've expressed praise and gratitude to a staff member, volunteer, donor, or business partner, I want to encourage you to double, even triple, your efforts. As long as your expressions remain sincere, increasing the frequency improves, not diminishes, the power and effectiveness of the expressions.

I never heard my staff say, "Tom, you're expressing too much praise for the work I'm doing to build our caregiver program." I never heard a donor say, "I'm tired of the handwritten cards and photos the wounded veterans in your program are sending me to thank me for my contribution." And I never heard one of our business partners say, "Please stop coming by to shake my hand to express your gratitude for all the in-kind gifts we provide."

Take the time and make the effort to express praise and gratitude to everyone connected with your organization. Then do it again, and again, and again.

Make it personal
The most powerful way to acknowledge someone is in person. In many instances, the only time board members and staff have a chance to thank

their supporters is at a fundraising or programming event. These places are appropriate, but there is no substitute for the impact of a private, one-on-one thank-you.

Encourage your volunteer coordinator to take your top volunteers out for a coffee, or invite them to a workshop on leadership. If your only chance to meet donors is at a fundraiser, make an effort to pull them away from the noise and bustle, and spend a few minutes thanking them for their support. Invite a few staff out for a bike ride after work and take a moment to praise them for their hard work and dedication when you stop for a water break.

Expressions of praise and gratitude should feel significant, genuine, and personal. To do that, be specific. "Alison, I want to thank you so much for all the work you did to decorate the bus for the Labor Day parade. Your artistic talent is amazing and I know all the spectators noticed our bus thanks to your hard work and creativity. It was a huge effort and I heard you even sacrificed a weekend with your family to complete the task on time. The result is an indelible memory and the kids can't stop talking about it. You're an inspiration to all! Thank you!"

One of my favorite acts of expressing gratitude is to cook dinner for major donors. To make the setting more convenient and comfortable, I usually cook the meal at their homes. Dinners are simple and light. For starters, I'll open a nice bottle of wine and serve a variety of gourmet cheeses, fruits, and crackers. If they like fish, I'll grill some halibut or salmon steaks, accompanied by a small salad and a vegetable or two. For dessert, I'll serve a small amount of sorbet or homemade ice cream.

Dinners are two hours or less and I center the majority of conversation on *their* hobbies, interests, and families. When the moment is right, I let them know how grateful I am for their financial support. I'll also show a short video of the work they're supporting so they can see the impact their social investment is making. The videos always make an emotional impact and prompt lively discussion about their commitment and ways they can get more involved.

When saying our goodbyes for the evening, I thank the donors one last time for their contribution and support. Then, as a surprise, I give them a high quality, beautifully framed photo of one of the programs or program participants their funds supported. It's a nice touch, big hit, and the photo provides a constant visual reminder of the good work they're supporting. It also provides an attractive conversation piece they can use to spark discussion about a program they support when friends stop by.

Hosting intimate dinners like these will set you apart from the majority of chief executives, development officers, and board members raising money. Major donors tell me over and over, "No one has ever made us dinner before!" and "You made us feel so appreciated—and special!"

You have choices. If you do little to express praise and gratitude, expect little support and donations in return. If you want big-time support and donations, get personal with your expressions of praise and gratitude and do it in a way that's genuine and memorable.

Perform acts of service and kindness
One way for managers and board members to make staff feel valued and appreciated is through small acts of service and kindness. They don't have to be extravagant or expensive, just meaningful and selfless.

For example, when I had a staff of five, I'd occasionally make them lunch, bring them coffee from Starbucks, or buy flowers and plants for their desks. Homemade cookies and toffee were very popular. I also made an effort to spend one-on-one time with each staff to help them with their work and to provide guidance in their quest to achieve personal goals and professional aspirations.

Whatever acts of kindness your leaders choose to do for staff and volunteers, encourage them to do things that will make people feel valued and appreciated.

As I mentioned earlier, one of the most generous acts of kindness you can offer staff is flextime. Flextime removes the traditional time constraints of an 8-to-5 job (i.e., one-hour lunches and two 15-minute breaks), so staff may pursue personal interests and appointments during the workday without being confined by a work clock.

I created a flextime policy at SVAS to encourage staff to exercise for two or three hours at lunch, enjoy a morning of powder skiing, spend time with spouses, go to a doctor's appointment, or leave early on a Friday to go camping. Whatever time they took off beyond an hour and a half, they needed to make up by staying later in the day, or by coming in earlier the next morning.

Flextime validates the hard work of staff, and shows them you respect their personal lives and interests. If you've never offered flextime as a perk, I suggest trying it to experience the positive impact it has on morale and productivity.

As the number of staff grows, it becomes more and more cost and time prohibitive to perform various acts of service and kindness. For example, when you have a staff of five, it's easy to make everyone lunch or take everyone to Starbucks. But with a staff of 20, it's more difficult, but not impossible, to make good on these types of perks. For example, instead of going to Starbucks, you could arrange to have a few urns of Starbuck's coffee delivered, and instead of making lunch, you could have a catered lunch delivered.

No matter how large your nonprofit becomes, it's important to remain committed to performing acts of service and kindness for your staff—and others! If you do, they will remain committed to you with joyful hearts and loyal service.

Empower staff and volunteers

One of the most powerful ways to express praise and gratitude is to empower staff and volunteers in their jobs. Once you've hired talented staff and trained quality volunteers, you need to trust them to do the work they were hired and trained to do. No one wants a controlling boss that nitpicks and micromanages. That's a surefire way to erode culture and discourage commitment.

To empower staff, start by providing them a sense of independence in their work. Establish specific outcomes you expect staff to accomplish and then allow them to create their own strategies, tactics, and work styles to achieve the outcomes. Managers can still maintain a level of involvement and oversight by providing occasional training, review, guidance, and inspiration.

Managers can also empower staff by supporting their professional aspirations. This can be done by paying for professional magazines, continuing education classes, instructional seminars, in-house presentations, and industry conferences.

You can also set up similar empowering structures for your volunteers and board members. What's most important is that the leaders of your nonprofit make a commitment to empower everyone with the tools and freedoms they need to do their jobs and fulfill their responsibilities efficiently and effectively. Doing this sends a clear message to those inside and outside the walls of your nonprofit that your nonprofit values people and appreciates their support, effort, and contributions.

Takeaways

A volunteer may not admit she likes praise, a donor may not expect a thank-you card, and an office manager may not ask for a day off, but each will be grateful when you extend a token of praise and gratitude to show your appreciation for the contributions they've made.

Deep down people want to feel appreciated for their contributions, if only moderately so. It's not because of pride or ego. Rather, it's a deep sense of wanting to feel their contributions are valued and significant and, in some cases, a feeling *they* are valued and significant.

Acts of praise and gratitude do not have to be big or flamboyant. Small, personal, and genuine expressions are far more meaningful and lasting. Make it a priority for all staff, board members, and volunteers to do more of the little things that validate people and their contributions. The response will be a deeper sense of commitment and loyalty of those passionate about building a gold standard nonprofit and fulfilling your mission.

Think of running your nonprofit like a 1950s mom and pop hardware store. When your staff and donors are sitting at the local diner, sipping coffee and eating apple pie, you want them to say things like, "My manager goes the extra mile!" "I've never felt so appreciated in my job." "Wow, the staff is so friendly and nice!" "The managers always greet me when I arrive and thank me when I leave." "Even the owner is helpful and considerate." "I love shopping there!"

No matter what lifecycle stage your nonprofit is in, make a commitment to establishing yourself as a likeable and thoughtful nonprofit as much as a "professional" nonprofit. When you think you've expressed enough praise and gratitude to the people supporting your efforts, no matter what their level of contribution, express it again . . . and again . . . and again!

CHAPTER 10

Accountability

Taking responsibility to deliver the goods

I n the for-profit world, the principle of accountability is fundamental and widespread. The business mantra is to grow sales, trim expenses, and improve efficiencies, all to increase earnings and profitability. Employees and board members understand if they don't do an effective job running their businesses and managing the bottom line, competitors are standing close by happily willing to take their market share.

In contrast, accountability is largely a murky word in the nonprofit world. The term conjures up images of stoic corporate cultures where employees punch clocks, work for autocratic bosses, and step on each other to meet quotas and climb corporate ladders.

Nonprofit cultures may be grounded in selfless service and compassionate management, but they are corporations and function like their for-profit equivalents in more ways than you might imagine. Nonprofits have boards and staff, own assets, raise money, and offer programs, products, and services. They pay taxes, report to the IRS, and follow local, state, and government regulations.

Of course, there are differences. The biggest is how a nonprofit uses its assets, including the money it raises. Government regulations state a nonprofit must use its assets to advance the cause or provide the service (the mission) for which the nonprofit business was created as determined by its board of directors. In a for-profit business, money raised, revenue generated, or profits earned go to the owners of the corporation.

The public "invests" money in nonprofits expecting "social returns" on their investments, so why shouldn't nonprofits be held accountable to deliver on their promises like for-profit corporations?

Why shouldn't the public expect nonprofits to have measurements of success to track outcomes and measure effectiveness? Why shouldn't staff and board members of nonprofits have performance objectives?

Why shouldn't donors receive statements showing the types of returns they're getting on their social investments?

I've read a lot of nonprofit literature over the years and I've never read anything suggesting leaders of nonprofits have the right to run their organizations without structure, accountability, or responsibility because they are doing noble work. I've also never read anything stating that board members and staff should receive passes for work performance and accountability as long as they're passionate about changing the world.

Yet, many nonprofits are afraid to adopt policies and structures to hold their board, staff, and organization accountable for goals, objectives, and missions they set out to achieve, and work they promise to deliver.

The truth is many nonprofits live in a world of double standards. They want their flextime, eco-friendly offices, and casual dress policies. They also want equal opportunity and equal access as their for-profit equivalents when it comes to funding, political clout, wages, benefits, perks, and publicity.

These nonprofits cry for equality, but they are often unwilling to be held accountable to show they *deserve* equality. It's as if they feel entitled to equality simply because they are selfless "charities" doing good work to save the world. Meaning, since they believe they have the hearts and passion of a Mother Theresa, why would anyone question their integrity or intentions?

Nonprofits with this mindset are in for a big surprise. Donors and foundations are more sophisticated than ever. Compassion and mission are still central to their motivation for giving, but donors are less and less willing to write checks simply for "good intentions." More and more, donors and foundations view their gifts as social investments and the nonprofits that provide the greatest returns will win the lion's share of their generosity.

Why is accountability important?

Accountability is a *First Things First* principle because every nonprofit, by law and moral obligation, is accountable to the public to deliver the social benefits and obligations they've promised to deliver.

When accountability becomes a cultural norm, a nonprofit begins to think in terms of quality, performance, outcomes, and impact. Concepts such as job performance, financial sustainability, ethical standards, operational efficiency, and program effectiveness are no longer ethereal goals. They become primary objectives and directives of a nonprofit and people's feet are put to the fire to ensure they get accomplished.

To be a gold standard nonprofit, make the principle of accountability a core value and cultural priority as early in your lifecycle as possible. First things first! If you do, you will spring past your competition to win the hearts, minds, and pocketbooks of supporters. Most importantly, you will build a community of trust and credibility, and feel confident you are fulfilling your mission with integrity in the most efficient and effective manner possible.

Case Study: Entitlement leads to complacency

When I left Sun Valley Adaptive Sports in the fall of 2010, we had 20 smart and passionate staff working to fulfill our mission. Everyone knew what to do, how to do it, and what was expected. Managers empowered their teams to do their jobs and manage themselves with little oversight. Our business rhythm was smooth, our programs were effective, and staff was happy.

Five years earlier, our business rhythm resembled a gyrating spool of constant change and chaos. We had three staff doing the work of six. Everyone wore multiple hats and worked around the clock to rebuild programs, raise money, acquire volunteers, and develop partnerships. The work was motivating and inspiring, but it was also exhausting and stressful.

Much of our effort at that time went to cleaning up the mess the former administration and board left behind. To get us back on track quickly, I set high expectations for our young staff and myself. As we started passing major milestones, I wanted to acknowledge and reward staff for their hard work and dedication, so I granted juicy perks and benefits.

I started by establishing a flextime policy so staff could set their own work schedules as long as they worked 40 hours a week. Next, I extended the number of paid holidays off from 8 to 14 and granted a paid day off for anyone who worked more than 50 hours a week. I also modified our maternity policy so staff with newborns could work from home.

By 2007, we had a staff of 10 doing the work of 15. Everyone was having fun, but working as hard as ever. The hard work paid off. Our wounded veteran program, Higher Ground, had become a national brand, capturing the attention of Pentagon officials, industry leaders, legislators, and national media.

To reward this incredible progress and success, I granted every staff an additional week of paid vacation and gave everyone a bonus equal to 10 percent of their salary. Also, any staff that was willing to work weekends to help run our wounded veteran therapeutic camps earned three days of paid time off per camp.

By the start of 2010, SVAS had a staff of 20. We worked hard and fell into a business rhythm that kept everyone busy, but not overworked. Staff was happy and job satisfaction was at an all-time high.

Then an unexpected opportunity changed everything. I was out to dinner one evening when a local real estate agent told me a small luxury hotel had just been listed for sale in Sun Valley. This was very exciting news because SVAS had been mulling over the idea of building a hotel-like retreat center to rehabilitate wounded veterans with traumatic brain injuries and post-traumatic stress.

The hotel was perfect. It was centrally located and had the tranquil and homey ambience of a classic Austrian chalet. It wasn't too big or too small. It had 29 rooms, three dining areas, a pool, Jacuzzi, sauna, weight room, conference center, and large, wheelchair accessible bedrooms.

The price was right, too. The owners were asking $7.2 million, almost half the price it was worth before the economy tanked. We figured the land alone was worth $7.2 million, but now we'd be getting the land, plus a beautiful, 30,000-square-foot boutique hotel with breathtaking mountain views.

The catch? The owners established a financing contingency requiring us to raise the funds in 90 days. The second catch? We needed to raise an additional $2.8 million for improvements and operating costs. The third catch? The board elected to absolve itself of any fundraising responsibilities related to the hotel and appointed me to raise all the funds and conduct a feasibility study. Lucky me!

It was a Titanic goal. The economy was in the throes of the worst recession since the 1930s and donors were closing their checkbooks as tight as clams in ice water. Actually, there was some good in all this. I had almost six months, not three, to raise the money because it took an additional 90 days to negotiate the purchase agreement that included price, building contingencies, and terms of acquisition.

To raise $10 million in such extraordinary circumstances required me to commit all my time and energy to raising money. This meant I had to disconnect myself from many other responsibilities, including oversight of staff and operations; not that I felt staff needed much oversight. I was running a culture steeped in entrepreneurialism and felt confident that the staff understood their responsibilities and was empowered with the tools and opportunities they needed to accomplish the work at hand.

About five months into the six-month fundraising window, a series of strange and startling events came to my attention. A parent called with a complaint about a volunteer neglecting her child at our kids' camp. A camp counselor called to express her concern about the lack of oversight and management at one of our adult programs, and one of our wounded veteran participants called and said he missed his flight because one of our staff forgot to take him to the airport.

These events were alarming enough, but other uncharacteristic events came to my attention. A foundation called to say one of the staff had missed a grant submission deadline. A major donor asked to volunteer, but no one returned his call. An intern came into my office to express her discontent with her internship experience. The bank called to say one of the staff, who was not supposed to be making bank deposits, was making deposits, and some of the staff had been taking unlogged time off.

All nonprofits make their share of mistakes, but when I noticed a spike in the number and severity of problems and complaints, I immediately took a couple of days off from my fundraising efforts to conduct an investigation.

Much to my chagrin, I discovered the staff I'd put in charge had simply checked out. For nearly two months, there had been little oversight of staff, programming, and operations. Accountability had morphed into irresponsibility and the old adage rang louder than ever, "When the cat's away, the mice will play."

The whole ordeal was embarrassing to say the least. I prided myself on hiring and training skilled and trustworthy staff, and the thought of something like this happening never entered my mind. But it did happen and I learned even the best staff can drift toward a culture of complacency when strong leadership and a culture of accountability are absent.

Fortunately, we ceased fundraising efforts for the hotel 20 days before the fundraising contingency deadline. Although I had pledges for nearly half the funds, the results of the feasibility study clearly showed the hotel was a bad investment, so we voted to terminate our efforts to buy the hotel.

It was a sad moment, but we put the hotel behind us and the staff and board turned its attention back to programming and operations, keeping the hope alive that one day we might be able to open a rehabilitation center for wounded veterans.

I quickly dialed back into my role as chief executive. My first order of business was discovering why things had gone awry during my time away and why some of the staff strayed so far from the standards of excellence they once esteemed.

I held one-on-one meetings with managers and three all-staff meetings. After a lot of candid discussion and some emotional moments, staff said it was their freedom that sent them wayward.

Without strong management to hold them accountable, it appeared some of the staff felt a sense of entitlement. As a result, they elected to swim in their perks and benefits while leaving their work, responsibilities, and commitment to the mission on the beach.

After everyone shared their feelings, thoughts, and apologies, I asked staff what they thought should be done to get us back on the gold standard track we had been following. They unanimously agreed on two things: managers should be held accountable to hold staff accountable for their work, and staff must achieve specific goals and objectives to earn luxury perks such as flextime and bonus days off.

Needless to say, our great team sprang into action. Everyone, including me, focused on the work at hand and the strategic objectives we set out to achieve. After a few months, we glided back into a smooth rhythm doing innovative programming that was capturing the attention of the nation. Once again, I was proud and happy, and the staff quickly earned back the perks they enjoyed so much.

The lesson of this experience is clear: if people are not held to standards of accountability, they may slip into a mode of entitlement and complacency and the quality of their work and the level of their commitment may diminish. It's an unfortunate truth, but people, by nature, tend to do what's convenient and feels good, not what's right and takes effort.

If you want to be a high-performance nonprofit, it's important to realize and establish structures of accountability in all areas of your business. This will keep you on track and true to your mission, and prevent complacency from taking a foothold.

Tactics and Tips
Create a culture of accountability

If you're in the startup phase, one of the first things you'll want to do is establish a culture of accountability. The best way to do this is for your founding board members to commit to the principle of accountability and make it a core value and a central governing component to all that is said and done to fulfill your mission. They should add the principle as a facet of your overall culture and then create policies and operational structures to manage and enforce accountability.

The earlier in your lifecycle your board can initiate this process the better. It can start by stating your organization's commitment to accountability and mindfulness in your bylaws and other governing policies. The board will also want to make sure it hires a chief executive and elects board members who believe in the principle of accountability, have track records exemplifying it, and are willing to enforce it.

Once adopted, the chief executive and managers will want to hire people with track records of accountability. They will also want to regularly remind staff and volunteers that your nonprofit believes in the principle of accountability and takes seriously the responsibilities it has to donors, beneficiaries, and constituents to deliver on the promises it makes.

If your nonprofit is two, three or 10 years old and the principle of accountability is not central to your culture, prepare for an uphill battle. Personal dynamics, organizational structures, and general resistance to change can cripple the process of adopting the principle of accountability, even if people believe the principle would improve effectiveness, funding, and image.

If you find yourself in this position, there is hope. Ask one or two influential and well-liked board members and the chief executive to help champion an accountability initiative. If they embrace the initiative, you'll be in good shape.

If they oppose it, start looking for a mediator with good rates, because you'll need one to manage the dogfight that will ensue as the demands for accountability by funders, board members, and quality staff mount.

Define the structure of accountability

Once you integrate accountability into your culture, you need to define how accountability will manifest itself in day-to-day operations. Start by sectioning major areas of accountability: board, staff, volunteers, programming, operations, and fundraising. Determine what responsibilities, tasks, and outcomes are important. Decide who (or what team or committee) should be held responsible for what.

You'll also want to define performance measures or measurements of success for each area of accountability you decide to track. Finally, you'll need to determine what consequences to enforce when people neglect their work, ignore their responsibilities, or fail to live up to an established set of behaviors or ethics.

Everything is fair game. For example, when addressing legal accountability, you'll want to consider a conflict of interest policy. When addressing bookkeeping accountability, you'll want to consider a check handling policy. When addressing fundraising accountability, you'll want to consider how much money board members will be responsible for raising.

Other areas of accountability include risk management, board member involvement, insurance protection, operational effectiveness, program growth, staff performance, and marketing efficiency.

If all this sounds like too many details and too much work, start with more general topics. Ask broad accountability questions such as, "Are we spending money wisely?" "Do we have safe operating procedures?" "Can we substantiate our claims about program effectiveness?"

What's most important when defining the structure of accountability is getting everyone thinking and acting in a *framework of accountability*. Once your nonprofit adopts a framework of accountability and applies it to people, procedures, policies, obligations, responsibilities, tasks, and outcomes, there is no limit to the success your nonprofit can achieve because you'll have a structure and a mindset in place to ensure that people deliver the goods they promised to deliver.

Board accountability

Board members are known for their eagerness to adopt the principle of accountability, but then failing terribly in their efforts to apply and enforce it. For example, most board members acknowledge they have a legal responsibility for the financial sustainability of their nonprofit, but few boards have accountability measures in place to ensure board members raise money, make financial contributions, and support the general fundraising efforts of their nonprofit.

A board may be able to neglect its fundraising responsibilities, but in other areas of business, neglect may result in an incident of "gross negligence" and lead to damaging publicity or a lawsuit. Boards have many serious obligations they are accountable to uphold, and it's the responsibility of the board to uphold them.

Do you have a conflict of interest policy? Has the board read it? Do they understand it? Do you have Directors and Officers insurance? Does the board understand what it covers and doesn't cover? Do you require each board member to read your IRS 990 each year? Do you have accounting measures in place to minimize the risk of embezzlement and misuse of funds?

Board accountability starts with the board chair. The board chair needs to actively and publicly fill his roles and responsibilities. He needs to walk the walk and deliver the goods. He should be a role model of accountability and encourage all board members to exemplify a culture of accountability in all the board says and does.

You should apply the same level of scrutiny when nominating board members as you would when electing a board chair or hiring a chief executive. As I said earlier, potential board members may be wealthy, connected, brilliant, and charismatic, but if they are unwilling to be held accountable for the responsibilities they take on, you're going to wind up with a sunken ship full of rusty treasure.

Be wise. Think of the long-term consequences of electing a set of board members unwilling to adopt a culture of accountability. Do you really want to face a multi-year, uphill battle resulting in personal confrontations, lost productivity, and missed opportunities?

Your board members are called nonprofit "trustees" for a reason; they hold "in trust" the trust of the public—those who support your nonprofit and those your nonprofit serves. Neglecting or dismissing fundamental board responsibilities, like accountability, puts your nonprofit at risk and does a moral disservice to the public.

However, if your board members—all of them—willingly adopt a culture of accountability and mindfulness early on and *everyone* remains enthusiastic and committed to fulfilling their roles and responsibilities, then you are in store for productivity and opportunity beyond anyone's expectations.

Board accountability questionnaire
Board members, as chief ambassadors of your nonprofit, should be accountable for fulfilling their responsibilities and knowing what your organization does. If you want to gain some insight into how much your board understands your nonprofit, pass out a short questionnaire like this one at your next board meeting:

1. How many board meetings did we hold last year? How many did you attend?
2. List each of our programs. How many did you observe in person last year?
3. Write a few sentences describing each of our programs and their purpose.
4. What is our mission statement? What is our vision? List as many of our core values as you can.
5. How many people did our programs serve last year?

6. How many volunteers do we have?

7. What is our budget for this year?

8. List our top 10 donors. List our top five business partners.

9. When was the last time you read our bylaws? Our 990?

10. When was the last time you read our conflict of interest policy?

11. How many public speaking engagements did you do last year?

12. Briefly summarize the history of the organization.

13. Briefly make a *case for support* why someone should donate to us, and why someone should volunteer to help.

14. List three responsibilities each board member must uphold. Did you fulfill these last year?

15. Apart from board meetings, how many hours did you volunteer for the organization last year?

The intention of this exercise is not to embarrass board members, though it will in some cases. It's designed to help board members realize how little they understand the nonprofit they "care so much about." Do not ask board members to hand in their answers or share them out loud. Rather, extend some grace and provide each board member with a set of answers.

Accountability starts at the top. Be smart and cautious! Take as much time as needed to elect board members willing to work hard, understand the organization, and be accountable for the responsibilities and tasks they committed to deliver. Have zero tolerance for lip service slackers.

Chief executive accountability
Accountability at the top also applies to the chief executive. It's a business imperative that your chief executive lives and breathes accountability and has a history of personal and professional accountability.

It starts with the hiring process. The objective is clear: hire a seasoned chief executive who understands the roles and responsibilities of a chief executive and knows how to build and run an organization grounded in standards of accountability.

If you've already hired a chief executive but she doesn't believe in the principle of accountability, or lacks the experience to implement a culture of accountability, you need to work with her to establish a culture of accountability. If she is unwilling to make the necessary changes, you may need to let her go.

Once you have the right chief executive in place, it's the board's responsibility to work with the chief executive to set specific objectives for which the chief executive will be held accountable. The board should derive these objectives from the strategic plan, the executive's job description, work tasks, and defined roles and responsibilities.

The board should also hold the chief executive accountable by asking pertinent questions about pressing concerns. Experienced executives will not balk at tough questions or requests for detailed information because they know transparency and accountability go with the job.

However, boards typically underestimate the amount of work a chief executive has on her plate, so it's important that boards refrain from making random, last minute requests for detailed reports that take hours to produce, especially if the requests coincide with a special event, grant deadline, or travel plans.

In some cases, chief executives are willing to be accountable to the board, but unwilling to be accountable to the staff. This typically occurs when a chief executive has a big ego with a controlling, top-down style of management.

She may believe staff works for her (beneath her), so why should she be accountable to staff for things such as leadership, training, support, guidance, respect, and validation? Boards need to be on the lookout for rogue chief executives like this and be willing to take swift action to address this type of behavior, or take action to change executives.

Your chief executive is probably the most public and powerful person at your nonprofit. She can single-handedly make or break your success. Your board must give her adequate support and freedom to do her job and keep her happy, but she must also be held accountable to execute the responsibilities, plans, strategies, and tasks set forth by your board.

This will all be well understood by a star chief executive who has a track record of establishing and managing cultures of accountability. How does your chief executive rate?

Staff accountability

Consider your nonprofit blessed if both your board and chief executive believe in the concept of accountability and remain committed to establishing and managing a culture of accountability. However, all their efforts will be in vain if you have a group of nonchalant staff with little regard for accountability.

Staff is the engine of a nonprofit. They provide the key moving parts that keep a nonprofit operating smoothly. They run programs, execute strategic plans, and manage operations. They talk with business partners, intervene with parents, and care for beneficiaries. They are front and center in the public's eye and are often the biggest champions of a nonprofit's mission. If they do their jobs well, everyone wins. If they do their jobs poorly, everyone notices.

As obvious as it sounds, the ability of your nonprofit to efficiently and effectively fulfill its mission and achieve success is directly correlated to your staff's ability to do their jobs well. The best way to ensure this happens is to hire quality staff and hold them accountable to fulfill their responsibilities and achieve objectives.

Finding quality staff can be difficult and tiresome, but as any seasoned manager will tell you, it's better *not* to hire someone than to hire the wrong person. To hire a team of star performers, start by writing clearly defined job descriptions and expectations. Screen candidates for track records of exceptional performance and accountability.

If they're young, ask questions about their involvement in sports, social groups, church, and odd jobs. Request they work for your nonprofit for a few days (paid), so you can observe their work habits, personality, and character traits. Take your time to get the right people in the right seats on your bus. Remember, it's much more difficult to fire someone than to hire someone.

Once you have your winning team in place, it's the responsibility of management to hold staff accountable for the work they are expected to perform. The chief executive and managers must establish work expectations through detailed job descriptions and measurable objectives established in a strategic plan, operational plan, fundraising plan, or programming plan.

Management should include staff in the development process of these plans. The chief executive should ask key staff to participate in the strategic planning process. Those involved in programming should help develop the programming plan. Those involved in operations should help develop the operations plan, and so on.

Management should also include staff in the process of setting staff work goals and objectives. I held one-on-one meetings with each of my key staff to review their goals, objectives, and performance for the current quarter and then established new goals, objectives, and performance measures for the upcoming quarter.

Before our meeting, I'd send an email asking key staff to prepare six or seven goals or objectives they would like to achieve. Sometimes I'd send prompting questions such as, "What three things can you do in the next three months to improve the work you're doing?" "What two things would you like to learn that will help you do your job better?" "What's one thing you can create in the next month to improve the quality of service we provide our participants?"

I'd often toss in a couple of personal questions as well, "What's one thing you'd like to accomplish that will improve your quality of life outside of work?" "What's one thing you could do to lower your stress?" "What's one thing you could do to improve a friendship you cherish?"

We'd discuss the answers, make modifications if needed, and agree on a final set of goals and objectives. Each staff would then be responsible to manage their goals and objectives with occasional encouragement and guidance from me or a manager.

By involving staff in the process of setting their own performance goals, they felt a greater sense of ownership and empowerment. They also felt more motivated to achieve their goals and, most importantly, felt more *accountable* to achieve them.

Staff accountability begins with getting the right people on board from the start. Don't settle for mediocrity! Be selective. Take your time and you will eventually find talented staff with exceptional track records of personal and professional accountability. The result will be a winning team driven by excellence to build a winning nonprofit.

Volunteer accountability

Many nonprofits would not exist if it weren't for the dedication and effort of committed volunteers freely offering their time, skills, and expertise. As vital as volunteers are to the success of a nonprofit, selecting them is tricky. Volunteers come in all shapes and sizes, and every volunteer feels he or she has something of value to contribute to their chosen nonprofit.

The problem here is the term "value"; it's a subjective term and the value of volunteers sometimes turns out to be more of a hazard than a benefit. For example, one of your volunteers might say he is an "expert" handyman, but it turns out he doesn't even know how to use a power drill. Volunteers can also be lazy, apathetic, rude, and irresponsible, and it's not uncommon for volunteers to show up late to important events, or not at all.

Nonprofits can solve many of their volunteer issues simply by establishing structures of accountability, but many nonprofits are unwilling to do this because they feel structures of accountability, such as written job descriptions, should not be placed on people who graciously donate their time and effort.

Actually, the opposite is true. Volunteers appreciate structure because they want to know what's expected of them. The job of a volunteer coordinator is to ensure these expectations are met by matching a volunteer's time availability and talents with the needs of the nonprofit, and by establishing tasks and responsibilities for which the volunteer will be held accountable to perform and fulfill.

The way to do this is through detailed job descriptions, thorough orientation, and ongoing training. Once these are in place, it's easier to manage the process of volunteer accountability as it relates to job performance, participation, and impact.

It's important for a volunteer coordinator to screen volunteers as thoroughly as managers screen staff. The coordinator should learn the details about a volunteer's work habits and character traits. Do they have a track record of completing tasks, showing up to work on time, and taking initiative? Will they be a good "fit" with staff, volunteers, participants, and the work you're asking them to perform?

Whether your volunteers help out daily, or once a year, they need to know volunteering for your nonprofit is a serious responsibility. Volunteers must understand you've set standards of performance and have a system in place to hold them accountable for the jobs and contributions they signed up to deliver.

This is a delicate thing to balance. On the one hand, it's important to get volunteers excited and motivated about the benefits they will receive by contributing their time, money, and expertise to further your cause, and on the other hand, you need to ensure their contributions actually provide a quality benefit to your nonprofit.

It's your job to manage the placement of the accountability fulcrum by selecting and training a team of volunteers that genuinely believes in your mission and is willing to be held accountable to help you fulfill it.

Imposing consequences
Okay, let's come out of the clouds for a minute. It's unrealistic to think every board member you elect, every staff member you hire, and every volunteer who signs up will fulfill every responsibility and complete every task in a manner expected of them.

So, how do you approach a board member who is your top fundraiser, but fails to attend board meetings month after month? What actions do you take against a chief executive who constantly passes her work off to staff? What do you say to a program manager who is loved by participants, but can't complete her paperwork on time to save her life? And what do you do with a volunteer who helps 20 hours a week, but walks around with a chip on his shoulder and criticizes the efforts of others?

These are difficult situations to manage. We all know it's much easier to establish guidelines of accountability than to enforce them. Even the most seasoned managers know it's difficult to confront someone who fails to do his job or fulfill a responsibility because any type of confrontation has the potential to get "personal." No one likes to hear she is doing a poor job or should improve her behavior, and certainly no one likes to get fired or be asked to stop volunteering.

I think it's true to say, many nonprofit executives and managers avoid inflicting consequences on others because they have soft hearts and are too nice—and often too afraid—to engage in any type of confrontation.

No one wants to be branded as a "mean manager," do they? This alone deters many softhearted managers from enforcing accountability and engaging in a confrontation because *they* fear getting hurt in the process.

There are many other reasons why leaders at nonprofits are unwilling to hold others accountable. A board chair might be unwilling to confront a fellow board member about raising money because the board chair may be a longtime business associate of the board member and is afraid of jeopardizing the relationship if the confrontation goes sour.

Volunteer coordinators find themselves in similar positions. They are often personal friends of volunteers. It can be very difficult to tell a friend that his behavior at the last children's event was so inappropriate that he must resign. The moment will be uncomfortable, but even more so when they see each other at a neighborhood picnic the following week.

It's disappointing and frustrating when staff and volunteers constantly fail to do their work or fulfill their responsibilities. What's worse is when leaders and managers tolerate poor behavior and work habits, and fail to impose consequences to address such issues. If enough leaders manage with this type of complacency, it will result in sloppy work, indifference, and insubordination that eventually erodes a nonprofit's culture and mission and all it hoped to achieve.

It's important you develop a caring and compassionate culture. It's also important that your leaders be sensitive and understanding when addressing those who fail to fulfill responsibilities and provide opportunities for improvement when mistakes are made. But just because they are caring and sensitive doesn't mean they have to be meek and tolerant. Your leaders must be held accountable *to hold others accountable* and to impose consequences when people come up short.

Takeaways

Establishing a culture of accountability does not have to feel like you're doling out jail sentences or turning into a bureaucratic for-profit organization run by autocratic thugs. If implemented delicately and managed well, accountability can be an inspiring principle to keep people engaged, productive, and honest. It can also motivate people toward a higher standard of excellence, nudging your nonprofit closer to fulfilling its mission by establishing a measurable sense of purpose.

Most importantly, a culture of accountability can preserve public trust. It provides a framework for a nonprofit to deliver on its promises in good faith with defensible management and governance practices.

Make a commitment to adopt and apply the principle of accountability. Start by electing board members, hiring staff, and bringing on volunteers who have personal and professional track records of accountability and believe in its merits.

Next, establish structures of accountability throughout your nonprofit. If you expect people and the organization to be held accountable, you need to establish well-defined job descriptions, responsibilities, objectives, goals, tasks, plans, and outcomes—for just about everything.

The last directive, and perhaps the most vexing, is establishing structures that hold leaders and managers accountable to manage accountability with compassionate hearts, yet be willing to impose consequences when staff, board members, and volunteers fail to live up to the work tasks, job responsibilities, and performance measures they've agreed to uphold.

Some in the nonprofit world believe, "We're doing this work because we're passionate about a cause, so stay off my back and let me have some fun." Nonprofits do serve a "social" purpose, and board members, staff, and volunteers should have fun while serving their chosen nonprofits.

However, this doesn't excuse people from being held accountable to do the work they committed to do to accomplish the mission they claim to care about so passionately. Adopting and managing the principle of accountability and all its associated structures will be one of the most daunting challenges you'll face at any time in the life of your nonprofit.

Unfortunately, many nonprofits are unwilling or too afraid to institute a culture of accountability. This gives you the opportunity to separate yourself from the ordinary nonprofits to be a great nonprofit—a gold standard nonprofit. To succeed, you must be willing and courageous enough to do what's right, not what's convenient. What path will you choose?

CHAPTER 11

Measurable Performance and Impact

Proving your worth

Most of America's 1.0 million nonprofits (those classified as charities) are considered "small." More than 80 percent have annual budgets less than $500,000. More than 90 percent have annual budgets less than $2 million.

Though the majority of nonprofits may be small in size and budget, their Mighty Mouse muscles tackle society's toughest social, medical, educational, cultural, and environmental challenges. They employ millions of people, provide thousands of programs and services that help millions more, and make the world a better place.

I'm a big fan of small nonprofits. I marvel at their agility and tenacity to make powerful and lasting changes in ways large nonprofits can't. They are the soul of the world's most noble work.

I'm also a tough critic of small nonprofits. When you look behind the curtain, you quickly notice that many operate like college intern projects—novel ideas, great hopes, and lots of passion, but little knowledge or practical experience of how to transform hopes and dreams into realities. The result is ineffective programming, inefficient operations, and careless management.

You certainly don't want to run your nonprofit like a haphazard intern project, but the good news is you also don't need an MBA or 20 years of nonprofit experience to run a gold standard nonprofit.

What you need is a team of authentically passionate people committed to working hard and thoughtfully to build and improve a nonprofit grounded in best practices, accountability, performance, and impact. Do this and you'll be light-years closer to success than the thousands of nonprofits that whimsically glide along with little focus and direction.

Why is measurable performance and impact important?

If your mission is not making an impact, why are you in business? If your programs and operations are performing well, how can you prove it? Measurable performance and impact is a *First Things First* principle because it validates your claims—and your supporters' expectations— that you are *truly* making a difference. Simply put: if you can't measure progress and success, how do you know if you have achieved it?

One of the biggest mistakes nonprofits make is underestimating the importance donors place on performance and impact. Donors once made donations to support causes. Now they view their donations as social investments to solve society's problems. When smart donors give money, especially major donors and foundations, they expect a nonprofit to show them what type of social returns the nonprofit will produce with the money it receives.

The key word here is "show." Most nonprofits do a great job of "telling" donors they are making a difference, when donors want nonprofits to show and *prove* they are making a difference, including how they are improving operations, fundraising, and management.

In the business world, measuring performance and impact is fairly straightforward because there exists a common currency for making comparisons—money. If you want to know how one company is performing relative to another, you compare standardized performance measures such as sales revenue, gross margin, profit margin, earnings per share, and return on investment.

Making performance comparisons in the nonprofit world is much more difficult. Nonprofits function to create change and there is no common currency for one nonprofit to compare its "social performance" to other nonprofits with similar missions, or even less so to nonprofits with different missions.

For example, how do you measure and compare the performance, impact, and success of a hunger relief organization such as Feeding America to that of the YMCA, United Way, or the World Wildlife Fund? Which is making a bigger impact? Which is performing better? Which is most successful? How do you make a fair comparison? You can't.

Scholars and pundits have been grappling with this issue for 40 years trying to figure out common currencies by which nonprofits can compare themselves. To date, there are a number of competing theories and models, but all have their flaws and none are widely used.

Fortunately, you don't need to be a scholar to measure performance and impact to prove you're a success. By tracking a few basic elements of your programming, operations, and fundraising, you can dazzle donors, validate your mission, and set yourself apart from the majority of nonprofits that fail to do the same.

Case Study: Small successes lead to big successes

At the time I rescued Sun Valley Adaptive Sports, it had no meaningful measures of success. Its summer day camp program reminded me more of a daycare program than an adaptive sports program. There were no goals for participants, no tools to track progress, and no systems to measure performance, impact, or success. Participants were having a lot of fun, but whether they were having a "therapeutic" experience, as the program claimed, was questionable.

The original SVAS program to help wounded veterans operated similarly. It ran like a Club Med—big on sports and partying, but short on therapy and substance. In some ways, the entire organization operated like a party. The office was a mess. Programs were disorganized and staff stumbled about without direction.

I continue to bring up the former SVAS administration and their wing-it style of management because it's such an easy target. The entire philosophy behind how SVAS once operated represents a model of how *not* to run a nonprofit, manage staff, raise money, engage volunteers, develop a board, involve a community, and treat participants.

I hope you learn from SVAS' blunders and make wise decisions to avoid the same misfortunes.

As the new chief executive, one of my first objectives was to establish a set of performance measures for every area of programming and operations. I knew once we did this, it wouldn't take long to see the impact of our new programming, and we'd soon be on our way to attracting committed volunteers and generous donors.

To start the process, I worked with the board and staff to determine what success would look like for the organization. I also wanted to define success for each primary functional area: programming, administration (operations), and fundraising.

We kept the process simple and meaningful. We wrote three measures of success and impact for each functional area. For example, our goals for programming were: 1) increase the number of hours children were able to ski in a season, 2) involve parents, teachers, and social workers in the design of therapeutic goals for the children, and 3) add more therapeutic components to our wounded veterans program.

We then set up systems to monitor and track progress for each measure of success. For example, to increase the number of hours children were able to ski in a season, we worked with Sun Valley Resort to secure season ski passes for all the children. The Resort was very gracious and offered season ski passes to each of our 80 children for only $25, a $375 value per child and a program savings of $30,000.

Previously, children in the program skied only four times a season. It's difficult to get good at any sport if you only do it four times a year. With a season ski pass, children could now take adaptive lessons from us twice a week and then ski with friends and families on the weekends. This encouraged more skiing at a fraction of the price.

We tracked the number of hours children skied with our instructors and the number of hours they skied with family and friends. By the end of the season, some children had skied 160 hours, a tenfold increase over the previous season.

We also tracked improvements in skiing ability, social interaction, and self-confidence. At the end of the season, we evaluated our findings and published the results. We also collected more than a dozen testimonials from school social workers and parents, and produced a beautiful DVD showcasing the children's progress throughout the season.

All this led to widespread support from families, donors, and the community. They read the statistics, reviewed our performance measures, and saw the impact. In the eyes of parents, we had proved beyond doubt the program was a success and made a positive and a lasting impact on their children. Parents and donors responded with gratitude and their checkbooks. By the start of the following season, the number of volunteers for the ski program doubled and fundraising tripled.

We followed a similar pattern of measuring success for each major program and functional area. We established simple and meaningful measures of performance, impact, and success and then created simple and meaningful methods to track progress. We collected data, evaluated it, and then published the results in a compelling manner.

Each year, as our budget grew and the number of our staff increased, we set loftier definitions of success for each program and functional area, and improved the systems used to measure and track performance.

By 2007, SVAS was a national leader in the world of adaptive sports therapy and, as I've said, many in our industry considered our programming "the gold standard." Dozens of organizations wanted to know how we ran our programs, how we tracked performance and outcomes, and how we measured success and impact.

We started working with universities and military medical hospitals to develop innovative ways to refine various rehabilitation therapies to improve the long-term care and restoration of wounded veterans and their spouses.

We were asked regularly to share our methods and findings at conferences and hospitals around the country, and I flew to Washington, D.C. twice a year to share our results with Veterans Administration officials, state legislators, and the Department of Defense.

Most importantly, the information we were tracking, compiling, and sharing was now helping enrich the lives of tens of thousands of wounded veterans and people with disabilities around the country. It was also improving the quality of service of hundreds of organizations working to serve these populations.

Our efforts did not go unnoticed by our donors. We earned credibility and their respect by *proving* our innovative work was making a tremendous impact. To reward our efforts, donors flooded us with $1.5 million that year to expand our wounded veterans program. This was three times more funding than we had raised the previous year.

What started as a simple objective to improve program quality, measure performance, and demonstrate success, turned into something much, much bigger. We ended up shaping the landscape of two industries and changing the lives—sometimes directly, sometimes indirectly—of tens of thousands of people, and raising millions in support. That's impact!

No matter how large or small your nonprofit is, you have a responsibility to your supporters, primary beneficiaries, and yourself to show your noble work is making a meaningful impact. The sooner you make this your primary goal, the sooner you'll be on your way to becoming a gold standard nonprofit that achieves its dreams. First things first!

Tactics and Tips
Define performance and impact
Before you can track performance and impact, you need to define it. You need to determine what types of performance measures and impact will be significant and what success will look like when you achieve it. Performance and impact will vary greatly depending on your mission and the interests of your board and management.

Set up a meeting with your board and key managers and start brainstorming how you'd like to define success, impact, and meaningful performance measures for programs, administration, fundraising, and your nonprofit. For example: "Starting an endowment by next January." "Improving our image in the community." "Increasing the number of adult literacy classes we offer by 40 percent in two years." "Doubling the amount of time our participants spend with our autism therapists."

The level of detail isn't as important as starting the process. Commit to defining measures of performance, success, and impact as early in your lifecycle as possible; you can modify your definitions and create new ones as your nonprofit grows and evolves.

Establish tracking methods
Once you've established a set of performance measures and measures of success and impact, you'll need to develop simple and meaningful methods to track each measure. Basically, a tracking method can be any systematic process used to track the progress of a performance measure, or track the measure of success and impact.

For example, if one of your performance measures is raising $30,000 a month in donations, you could track progress by tallying bank deposits, or by adding donation amounts you've entered into your donor database. Either method will give you the same result. What's most important is establishing a set of tracking methods so you can track the progress of the performance measures you defined.

If you're a small nonprofit, you're probably short on funds, so make sure you establish *affordable* tracking methods that are still efficient and effective. Meaning, why would you use a tracking method costing $500 in labor when an alternative method is available at half the cost and provides the same results?

You'll also want to be on the lookout for the hidden costs required to manage tracking methods. It's easy to overlook the time and resources needed to collect, process, and evaluate data, and the costs associated with meetings, training, software, and printing. It all adds up. If you're not careful, the time and money you spend to track success may disrupt your ability to create it.

Should you use evidence based research?
After a few years in the nonprofit world, you quickly learn many donors and foundations use "evidence based research" as a standard by which they judge programming performance and impact.

Evidence based research works best as an evaluation tool for large organizations operating in established industries such as health care and education because so much efficacy research takes place in these industries. The opposite is true in most small nonprofit sectors. Research is sparse and many nonprofits don't fit neatly into a particular industry, or they provide services to a number of industry sectors.

Nonetheless, many old-school donors and foundations believe evidence based research is the only tool to effectively evaluate nonprofits. It's your job to show people you can still be a high-performance, impact-oriented nonprofit without having to hire scientists and statisticians to conduct and publish clinical research.

If you're a small or busy nonprofit, it's unlikely you have the money or time to conduct evidence based research. However, if you're in an industry that publishes research supporting the type of work you do or service you provide, you should tap into it. National associations and professional workgroups are great resources. You can use the results of their research to supplement your findings and validate your work. In the process, you may glean insights into ways to define your measurements of success and tracking methods.

Not all foundations and donors make unrealistic demands. Many are empathetic and supportive. They understand the growth pains and resource restrictions small and busy nonprofits face. They have expectations of performance and impact, but they are realistic about the time and resources required to produce it.

Most foundations and donors will fund you if they feel you are taking some degree of responsibility for tracking performance, measuring success and impact, and demonstrating that the money you receive is used *wisely*. To them, it's not about publishing piles of science and statistics, it's about meaningful effort and intention. These are the types of foundations and donors you want to seek out.

Substantiate your magic
Social change often occurs in unexplainable ways. Call it mystical, magical, or spiritual, but sometimes change happens in ways that are difficult to identify, explain, or duplicate.

For example, let's say John is a wounded veteran recovering from a gunshot wound to the head he received while serving in Iraq. Doctors say his traumatic brain injury limits his motor skills, and his post-traumatic stress is causing him to be short-tempered and depressed. Six times a day he takes painkillers and anti-anxiety medications. At night, John cannot fall asleep without heavy doses of sleeping pills.

John regularly expresses suicidal thoughts. He argues with his wife daily. He has been attending counseling at a Veterans Administration hospital for six months and has made no progress. As a result, John's counselor recommends John and his wife attend a SVAS therapeutic watersports camp for wounded veterans in Sun Valley.

They arrive in August and spend a week with six other couples at a remote alpine lake in the Sawtooth Mountains. All the couples have their own rustic cabins and their days are filled with thrilling sports and fun recreational activities. They talk with peers, make new friends, and take part in relaxing therapeutic exercises. The peace and tranquility of the mountains give John a chance to slow down and disconnect from his hectic life in the city.

By the end of the week, John says he has reduced his pain medication by two-thirds and no longer requires sleeping pills to fall asleep. He has made a commitment to renew his relationship with his wife and he will no longer allow his injuries to define his life. John also says he's decided to go back to school and learn more about technology with hopes of landing a job with the military in the area of national defense.

In John's words, "What happened in Sun Valley was 'magical.' I can't put it into words exactly, or pinpoint the moment, but I feel like a new person. I now have hope. I feel renewed. You've changed my life, and my wife and I will forever be grateful!"

What was it about John's experience that made it so transformational? Was it the moment he got up on water skis for the first time? Was it the staff therapist who listened to his pain without judgment? Was it creating an environment where John had a chance to talk to peers with the same injuries and similar combat experiences? Was it the tranquil surroundings that freed his mind? Did God intervene? Was it none of these things, or was it a little bit of all these things?

John's story is similar to the types of stories you hear at job training centers for single mothers, hunger relief organizations, or substance abuse programs. Magical things happen all the time and they are difficult to identify and quantify.

If someone has a life-changing experience because of the work you're doing, it's meaningless to get nit-picky about the methods used to quantify it. Whatever it was, it worked and that's what's most important.

Social entrepreneurs are driven by change, and the way they create it is often more magical than mathematical. If magic is a component of your nonprofit's success, it doesn't grant you a license for inefficiency and neglect. You'll still want to establish well-defined performance measures and measures of success and impact that substantiate your magic.

At the very least, you'll need to show your supporters how you create settings and methods that allow magical things to happen.

Justify expenses and target sensible ratios

The IRS requires you to track the amount of money you spend on programming, administration, and fundraising. You must submit these amounts each year when you complete your annual IRS 990 tax form. Most nonprofits also publish these figures in their annual reports.

As you begin fundraising, you're sure to encounter a small number of donors that believe *all* funds raised by nonprofits should go to programming and *any* money spent on administration and fundraising is wasteful. Some nonprofits do spend too much money on administration and fundraising, and some do waste money. Most don't.

Justifying expenses

What may be obvious and justifiable expenses to you may not be clear to your donors. It's your job to inform donors *why* you're spending money to rent office space, buy iPads, hire staff, lease office equipment, host lavish fundraising events, and pay for cell phone services.

On the other hand, money is in short supply for many nonprofits. It takes a lot of time and effort to cultivate new donors, write grants, and secure funding. This means you will most likely have to spend money on fundraising to raise money.

This creates a paradox: nonprofits want to develop quality programming and donors want to support quality programming, yet nonprofits get penalized for spending money on things such as administration, salaries, technology, and fundraising that allow them to create and manage quality programming.

The good news is most donors and foundations are sensible. They understand nonprofits must invest in resources to start a nonprofit and then invest again to expand programming, build operational capacity, and raise money. If you can justify your expenses and show they are *necessary and reasonable,* and help advance the efforts of your mission, you'll find that the majority of donors and foundations will give generously with few strings attached.

For example, let's say one of your donors is willing to fund a $70,000 salary so you can add a professional physical therapist to your staff. Before she writes a check, it's possible she will want to know if the expense is necessary and reasonable, and how a professional therapist will improve programming quality and propel your mission better than a slightly less experienced therapist at $40,000. Your job is to make a convincing case showing why the $70,000 therapist is a better value.

Your budget and financial statements provide the most amount of information about how you manage income and expenses. All foundations and most of your major donors will ask to see these documents in detail. The rest of your supporters will simply want to know, "What's your budget?" and "What's your fundraising goal?" But the one question you'll hear most often is, "What percentage of your funding goes to programming, administration, and fundraising?"

Targeting sensible ratios
This last question brings us to the topic of functional area ratios. Since so many foundations and donors place such a high value on these ratios, it's important you carefully track them and target sensible percentages.

What's sensible? For young nonprofits, or for those in an expansion phase, I suggest no less than 60 percent of funding go to programming, no more than 25 percent for fundraising, and no more than 25 percent for administration.

As a nonprofit settles into a business rhythm and expansion levels off, I suggest no less than 70 percent of funding go to programming (above 80 percent is exceptional), no more than 20 percent for fundraising, and no more than 15 percent for administration.

Of course, there will be exceptions. As an expanding nonprofit, you may need to make a large investment to hire additional staff to accommodate programming expansion, or you may need to beef up fundraising efforts to prepare for a major capital campaign. Neither increase is a problem as long as you inform donors and can justify your decisions.

One of the biggest criticisms surrounding the use of ratios is that they don't account for intangibles such as value and goodwill. Say you decide to hire a chief executive. At $50,000, you can get an executive who will do an adequate job, and the cost of her salary will allow your programming ratio to sit at 81 percent. This will leave your administration ratio at 10 percent and your fundraising ratio at 9 percent. Not bad.

Now, what if you paid $120,000 to hire a social entrepreneur superhero who can do the work of four staff, raise millions of dollars with ease, and turn everything she touches into gold? However, if you hire her, the cost of her salary will cause your programming ratio to sag to 65 percent. This will leave your administration ratio at 26 percent and your fundraising ratio at 9 percent.

Is she worth it? Would you be willing to tolerate a programming ratio of 65 percent? How would you justify your decision to donors who will think you've spent too much money on overhead?

Functional area ratios provide supporters with a lot of good information to make social investment decisions, but they also have their pitfalls. It's important you carefully track these ratios and target sensible percentages, but more importantly, you need to justify your expenses and show they are necessary and reasonable. If you can do this, you'll find plenty of generous donors willing to fund your worthy mission.

Takeaways

Are your programs successful? Is your fundraising effective? Are your operations efficient? Can you prove your programming is making a difference? Do you espouse a culture of innovation and improvement? Is your nonprofit a good social investment? Questions like these are at the forefront of every wise supporter's decision to fund you. It's up to you to prove your worthiness.

If you're a small nonprofit, it's likely you have neither the time, money, and in many cases, the experience, to prove your value and worthiness using complicated tracking methods, detailed performance measures, or expensive research.

Steer clear of the expense and frustration. To show you're a success, you need only establish a few *simple* measures of performance, impact, and success for each major functional area (including your nonprofit in general), develop reliable methods to track and evaluate key data, establish reasonable functional area ratios, and then publish the results in a clear and compelling manner.

As you grow and as resources permit, you can refine your methods and measurements of performance, impact, and success, and look for ways, if possible, to incorporate well-established industry research to supplement and substantiate your findings.

Finally, if your success includes magical or unexplainable components, you'll want to find ways to share these results and show their impact, if only through qualitative data such as testimonials of how you created an environment to facilitate your magic.

Keep in mind, more than 90 percent of America's 1.0 million nonprofit charities have budgets less than $2 million. Also keep in mind, many nonprofits lack the know-how to run an efficient and effective organization that can transform their dreams into realities.

Major donors and foundations know this. They want to create social change as much as you do and they are constantly on the lookout to fund nonprofits that can deliver the goods. To them, it's not how big you are, or how fast you're growing, it's how "deep" you are.

So, as you're flexing your Mighty Mouse muscles to create a gold standard nonprofit and change the world, make sure you *show* donors and foundations the impact you're making, so you can *prove* to them your passion and hard work are worthy of support. If you do, money and support will flow easily and generously.

CHAPTER 12

Technology
Leaping forward byte by byte

Technology continues to change the nonprofit world in unimaginable ways. No longer can a nonprofit sit quietly on the sidelines and say: "We don't need a great website." "We can't afford new laptops." "We don't have time to learn donor database software." "We don't need to take part in social networks." "Technology is too expensive."

More than ever, it's vital that nonprofits embrace many forms of technology to function efficiently and effectively, deliver high quality programs, stay connected, and remain competitive. If they don't, they will slip farther and farther behind those that do.

Also, today's workforce at most nonprofits is young and technologically savvy. They live in a realm of cloud computing, smart phones, iPads, "apps," databases, virtual communities, social networks, e-commerce, blogs, and webinars. Many college grads and young professionals have been using technology since grade school and insist on it so they can do their jobs well. Some feel crippled without it.

It's no longer a question whether you should adopt technology; it's imperative. The issue is what technology to adopt, when to adopt it, how much to spend, and how to manage it.

Why is technology important?
Technology is a *First Things First* principle because technology epitomizes efficiency, effectiveness, and leverage. Huge leverage! It can help simplify bookkeeping, create marketing materials, and raise money. It can increase productivity, reduce costs, and save time. Technology can also promote a brand, improve program quality, and deepen relationships with donors. Whatever task or responsibility you need to do, technology probably has a solution to help you do it better and less expensively.

Technology can increase productivity and create leverage, but it comes at a cost—opportunity cost. Nonprofits typically have resource constraints, so they must make cost-benefit decisions between technology and other purchases. "Do we buy iPads and iPhones for our field staff, or do we buy new program equipment for our participants?" "Do we buy a new contact database to manage donors, or do we hire another program coordinator?"

These are tough choices to make. On one hand, you must allocate resources to maintain adequate levels of support for core expenses such as labor, insurance, rent, utilities, benefits, programming, and supplies. On the other hand, you must embrace technology to remain competitive and maintain a high level of efficiency, effectiveness, and leverage.

Your job is to strike a balance between the two. Most importantly, you need to make a commitment to adopt a willingness to use technology to fulfill your mission as early in your lifecycle as possible, so you harness the benefits of technology as your capacity increases and when opportunities present themselves. First things first!

Otherwise, you may find yourself hamstrung by having no technology in place, having old technology in place, waiting too long to adopt the right technology, or being forced to adopt the right technology at an inconvenient time.

Case Study: Swimming in pools of irritation

Ebase was one of the earliest software programs developed to manage donor contributions and contact information. Developed in the 90s, tens of thousands of nonprofits used this clumsy software because it was free and because there were so few choices available at the time. More than two decades later, nonprofits still download Ebase's antiquated technology for no other reason than it's free.

More surprising is the number of mature nonprofits that continue to use Ebase. They refuse to spend $5,000 to buy a more sophisticated, easy-to-use program, yet they don't think twice about spending $10,000 a year on Ebase consultants to help them operate and maintain a bug-ridden program that constantly crashes and mysteriously loses data.

Like many nonprofits, Sun Valley Adaptive Sports chose Ebase as its donor database program because it was free. When I came on board, the program was a major source of frustration for the staff and they used it only out of necessity. I recall our office administrator saying, "Learning Ebase is as difficult as learning how to juggle—blindfolded." Simple tasks such as donor searches, mail merges, or bulk emails required a number of complicated, time-consuming steps.

In 2005, SVAS was spending $12,000 a year in Ebase consulting fees. Needless to say, using Ebase was a big waste of time and money, and during my first year at SVAS, we kept doling out money on Ebase consulting fees and swimming in pools of irritation.

That same year, the board nixed three staff requests to buy new software. Board members justified their decision by claiming staff was too busy restructuring operations and programming to have the time to adopt new software, and that the organization couldn't risk any type of disruption that might take place during the adoption process.

One afternoon in early 2006, I sat down to do what I thought would be a simple mail merge task involving three Ebase donor files. After dozens of unsuccessful attempts, I called our Ebase consultant for help. He was stumped too. After several unsuccessful attempts at contacting Ebase's technical helpline, I growled and said, "No more!"

The next morning, I called the board chair and pleaded my case for new software and the funds to buy it. By noon, the board approved my request. Over the next week, I had my operations manager read software reviews, call sales reps, and ask fellow nonprofits for recommendations. We quickly narrowed our choices based on price, functionality, ease-of-use, and technical support.

We settled on Giftworks. We bought the software online and in less than an hour, downloaded and installed the program, transferred all our donor data from Ebase to Giftworks, and were up and running.

The staff was thrilled! They raved about how easy Giftworks was to learn and use, and how powerful it was at managing data and generating reports. By the end of the week, we bought three more Giftworks licenses. It was the program we needed at a price we could afford. Cost: $1,600 ($400 per license). Plus, it included a year of free technical support.

I'm estimating here, but I suspect our Ebase woes were costing SVAS $25,000 a year when factoring in consulting fees, training, and maintenance, plus all the opportunity costs associated with lost productivity (staff wages) and aggravation due to database crashes and lost data. This figure is substantial when you consider our entire annual budget at the time was only $450,000.

After making the switch to Giftworks, I realized we had held onto our Ebase dinosaur for way too long. It was not only a waste of time and money, it was a waste of productivity.

I can only imagine what SVAS might have been able to achieve in the way of programming and fundraising had it not had to redirect hundreds of hours and thousands of dollars to deal with our Ebase afflictions.

No amount of excuses will help you justify a bad technology decision. Technology can be your best friend or worst enemy. To be a gold standard nonprofit, you must make wise technology choices.

Tactics and Tips
Find an expert and assess your needs
The first thing you need to do to ensure you have the right level of technology in place is to assess your technology needs and establish a technology plan. The last thing you want to do is to take a haphazard approach to adopting technology.

Buying random computers with little thought about functionality or compatibility will lead to agonizing problems that siphon away precious time and money year after year and give you one migraine after another.

Even if you have only a handful of staff and one or two small programs, it's essential you value the importance of technology early on in your lifecycle because the wise use of technology puts you in a better position to embrace growth, change, and opportunities as they present themselves.

To accurately assess your technology needs, you'll want to receive input from one or two chief executives who work in the same industry, and at least one information technology (IT) specialist. They can provide valuable insight into the types of technology solutions that work and how to avoid technology landmines.

Most executives, and a handful of IT specialists, will provide advice for free if the demand on their time is nominal. Otherwise, expect to pay a few hundred dollars for an afternoon of advice. It's worth it. Be sure to invite key staff to the meetings because they can best describe the details of how they do their work and the challenges they face.

The objective for the experts attending these meetings should be to listen to your programming and operational needs and challenges, and then suggest affordable, easy-to-use solutions that will help all areas of your nonprofit run more efficiently and effectively.

During the meetings, you'll want to discuss and address issues such as: What hardware, software, and communication technologies would provide the greatest benefit at the least cost? What technologies are critical to our programming success? Operations success? What types of technologies would we like to have, but can't afford? What technology is the best match for a given task? What technologies should we keep? Which need upgrading? Which should we replace? How much training will be required for each technology we adopt?

Once you finish the assessment process, ask the IT specialist to draw up a *simple,* one- or two-page technology plan. The plan should highlight the basics of what software, hardware, and communication technologies you should consider adopting, how long it will take to implement each technology, and how much you can expect each technology to cost. The plan should also include a section on training and maintenance.

The most important thing to remember about conducting a technology assessment is to conduct one early on in your lifecycle and to keep the plan simple. Focus on solutions that will be useful for the next 1-3 years. You'll have plenty of time to develop a more complicated plan as you grow and as resources permit.

Buy what you need, not what you want

Once you've assessed your technology needs and written a simple technology plan, you need to make purchases and begin the process of adopting technology.

The most important advice I can give you about buying technology is to buy what you *need,* not what you want or what you think you need. Avoid buying extravagant hardware, software, phone systems, cell phone packages, and "apps" that provide no practical benefit.

Keep in mind the classic 80/20 rule. It states: 80 percent of the time you'll use only 20 percent of the capability of the software and hardware you buy. From my experience, it's more like 90/10.

It's easy to get swept up in the hype of buying something new like a fancy graphics software program you think will help you build and manage a stunning website. Then, $600 later, you discover it's too complicated to use, no one has the time to learn it, and your offsite website designer already has a copy of the software.

Be smart. Buy technology that's easy to implement, easy to learn, easy to upgrade, and is scalable. Ask an IT specialist to help you make your purchases. They keep up on the latest industry trends and know what brands provide the best value for specific needs. This is their area of expertise, not yours, so give them a budget and let them work their magic.

Develop a social media presence . . . wisely!

Most of the principles above apply to social media sites as well. Some sites are good, some are not so good. Your job is to find sites that will best serve your needs, not necessarily sites that are popular.

Facebook, Twitter, LinkedIn, Instagram, and YouTube are just a few of the big guns in the social media world—for now, anyway. It can be nerve-racking to think about which sites to join and how to allocate resources to maintain a presence on each site.

It's estimated that a small nonprofit can spend up to 30 hours a week managing its social media presence. Since most small nonprofits are short on resources, it's important they make wise decisions about how to best use social media.

There are many factors to consider when choosing a social media site. I'm going to provide a few insights here, but for a detailed exploration of the topic, you should consult your IT guru or a social media expert.

Before joining any social media site, take a step back and ask some basic questions about what you're trying to accomplish through the site. Are you trying to advocate a position, communicate a message, build your constituent base, raise funds, or a little bit of everything? Whatever your reasons, make sure that one of your primary objectives is to engage and listen to your community.

After addressing these basic questions, you'll want to establish a strategy. Set realistic goals and clear objectives. Consider the time and cost needed to maintain your sites, and set up some type of evaluation methodology to track performance and measure success.

Five ways to ensure a strong media presence

1. *Tell more people.* Tell everyone at every opportunity about the social media sites you maintain and encourage them to join. Tell them in your communications material, on your website, in your email signature, and anytime you're speaking in public or in the media.

2. *Send frequent posts.* You want to post frequently, but not so much that it feels like spam. Avoid sending the same message out through all your social media sites. Redundancy is a turnoff.

3. *Post engaging content.* One of the best ways to capture—and hold—people's attention on a social media site is to create engaging content. When crafting messages and graphics, think to yourself, "Is this post engaging?" "Is it compelling?" "How will people react to this post?" "Will it motivate people to take action?"

4. *Talk back.* The essence of social media is two-way conversation. It's important to listen carefully, respond back, and facilitate dynamic conversation. This takes time. If you're not willing to invest the time, then your social media presence and effectiveness will eventually wither.

5. *Focus on your mission.* Keep your social media presence centered on your mission. If you start talking about your favorite pet instead of your programming, your visitors will lose interest.

Buy compatible systems

Macs and PCs are both good systems, but they are not compatible—though the manufacturers of both claim they are. Phooey! If you try to mix and match Macs and PCs, I guarantee you'll end up with the equivalent of technology food poisoning. Do not flirt with this disaster; buy compatible hardware and software you can easily install, network, and integrate.

Also, do not buy two different software programs to perform the same function. For example, don't buy Word *and* WordPerfect to do word processing, and don't buy InDesign *and* Quark Express to do graphic design. Buy one program to do one function and do the best you can to keep everyone updated with the same version.

Get networked

The power of technology shines brightest when it facilitates information sharing. There is no better way to do this in an office setting than to have everybody on a shared network. A well-designed network allows you to quickly swap emails, collaborate on documents, and share business contacts.

Nowadays, the smallest desktops have enough power to run software that can network a staff of 30. A WiFi network for small businesses is affordable and easy to manage. Have an IT specialist get you up and running with basic package that allows you to share printers and fax machines as well as files, emails, and business contacts. If your staff is in the field more than the office, consider a cloud-based network.

Set up your network as soon as possible. It may cost a few thousand dollars, but it will pay for itself ten times over within a year. The longer you wait the more costly and time-consuming the process will be when you finally make the conversion. Start smart. Network now.

Establish a secure backup process

People who started using computers in the early 80s have at least one horrifying story of losing all their data because their hard drive crashed. Today, the concern is viruses and worms. The reality of losing thousands of hours of work is mind-numbing. But the possibility is real. Lost data, and the time to replace it, can cost tens of thousands of dollars.

Don't wait. Buy the best backup system you can afford. This could be an external hard drive of some sort, or better yet, a cloud-based backup service. Both are convenient and easy to use. A quality backup system is one of the least expensive technology purchases you can make. It will also allow you to sleep deeply and nightmare free.

Hire tech-savvy staff

Training people to learn software, hardware, and network systems can be exceptionally costly and time-consuming. One of the smartest decisions you can make to avoid this resource drain is to hire people with strong technological skills.

Let's say you've decided to hire a new program director. The candidate you like best has 10 years of program related experience, but hardly any computer experience. Your second pick has only five years of program experience, but is a wizard in all types of software and hardware systems, is an active user of blogs and social network technologies, and has built her own website using a graphic design program.

Even though the first candidate has more program experience, I would hire the second candidate because people with strong technological skills know how to use technology to learn job functions quickly, and to do their work more efficiently and effectively. This assumes, of course, both candidates are closely matched in other areas.

Plus, if the second candidate already has strong technological skills, there is a good chance she can quickly learn the ins and outs of any technology she might need to perform her job responsibilities. Whereas, it could take months, perhaps years, for the first candidate to learn these programs and cost you thousands in training fees and lost productivity.

The good news is you don't need to choose between a candidate with job experience and a candidate with technological expertise. You can hire a candidate with exceptional job skills *and* exceptional technological skills. Your challenge is being patient enough to hire the right person.

It would be nice if every staff person you hired was a techie, but that's unrealistic. So, to keep your not-so-techie staff up-to-date with the latest advances in technology, you'll need to establish a budget and allocate time to train staff.

Think of technology training as an investment, not an expense, because a staff with strong technological skills provides double, sometimes triple, the job value of a staff with weak technological skills. And the more job value you direct toward your mission, the more likely you are to fulfill it.

Buy contact database software
You'll need to buy many different types of technology, but none will prove more valuable than the contact database software you use to track donors, donations, volunteers, and participants.

Fundraising staff use contact database software to make calls, set appointments, and manage donations. Volunteer coordinators use it to make calls, manage events, and assign tasks. Program coordinators use it to manage participant information, set appointments, and run programs.

Many small nonprofits don't use contact database software. They make the mistake of trying to manage names and information on paper, in word processing documents, or in a spreadsheet. These solutions will work for a while—a short while. Simple tasks managed in these formats quickly become complicated burdens once a nonprofit has a few dozen volunteers and a few hundred donors.

A more effective solution is to buy a contact database system. It doesn't have to be expensive or sophisticated, but you want to buy a program that allows you to easily access contact information, manage tasks, track donations, send email, generate reports, and share information.

Another one of my favorite contact databases is Bloomerang. It's inexpensive, easy to learn, simple to use, and the company provides excellent and accessible customer support. Try it . . . you love it!

It may take a few weeks to conduct the necessary research to find a high quality contact database program that fits your needs and budget. That's fine. What's most important is to find a good program and to start using it *before* you ramp up your efforts to acquire donors and volunteers, because the more people and information you're managing, the more time-consuming and expensive it will be to convert from one system to another down the road.

Consider overlooked, but important technology (for startups)
High-speed color printer
A high-speed color printer is an overlooked and very important piece of technology every nonprofit should own. We live in an age of eye-popping graphics, and graphic images lose their pop if printed on low-quality printers that produce smudged type and grainy photos.

A high-speed color printer allows you to mass-produce letters, reports, handouts, envelopes, flyers, and fact sheets without having to leave the office to outsource the work at a print shop. Of course, for print runs of 10,000 or more, it will be more cost-effective to outsource the work.

A quality, high-speed printer that prints 50 to 100 color pages per minute will cost $1,000 to $2,500. For a small nonprofit, this may seem like a lot of money to spend on a printer, but in the long run you'll get five times the performance at a fraction of the cost.

Laptops and tablets for all staff

Another one of the smartest technology purchases you can make to increase work productivity and job satisfaction is to buy every one of your staff a laptop or tablet. They are affordable, portable, and take up less room than desktops. These devices allow staff to work when traveling, or from home when sick. Staff can also use these devices to track participant data during programming activities and events.

Buying laptops and tablets may seem like an obvious recommendation in this day of affordable computers, but I'm always surprised how many nonprofits opt to buy bulky desktops to save a few hundred dollars. When you factor in portability, productivity, and user satisfaction, laptops and tablets are a much better value.

Donated technology

You're bound to receive used computers, printers, displays, phones, and tech gadgets from gracious donors. My advice is to respectfully decline such gifts unless the devices are in *excellent* condition and running the latest versions of software.

If not, they may cost you more in repairs and headaches than buying new devices. Thank the donor for his kind offer and then advise him to donate his device to a nonprofit that refurbishes used technology and sends it to developing countries.

Takeaways

Too often nonprofits take the position, "Let's wait until we're larger to buy a contact database program," "Laptops are too expensive," or "We can't spend time to manage our social media sites right now."

Nonprofits that take these positions and wait to adopt essential technology often experience one of the most painful and expensive lessons a nonprofit can learn—the larger you grow and the longer you wait to adopt essential technology, the more time, money, aggravation, and lost productivity it will cost once you decide to adopt it.

Call it Murphy's Law, but you can bet that when you decide to make a major technology change, it will come at an inconvenient time, usually right in the middle of a major growth spurt.

You can also bet that when you adopt a new technology, especially something as pervasive as a new server or new contact database software, it will come with a sack full of glitches, headaches, and setbacks. Bank on it.

The best way to reduce the impact of the unexpected is to hire an IT specialist to help you assess your needs, make purchases, implement the technology, and maintain it. Technology is not a do-it-yourself business.

You'll want to make sure you buy compatible systems, get networked, start using a good contact database system, and make wise choices when selecting social media sites and apps.

You'll also want to buy a high-speed color printer and you'll want to make a commitment to buy every one of your staff a laptop or tablet. If you haven't done these things, set a goal to make all these changes in the next year, even if it requires raising additional funds—it's worth it!

Arguably, the smartest technology decision you can make is to hire technologically literate staff and commit to an ongoing technology training program. The greater your staff's ability to use a variety of hardware, software, and communications technology, the more productive they will be doing their jobs and fulfilling your mission.

When technology is wisely purchased and correctly used, it's the ultimate tool of leverage. It can manage information for thousands of donors, volunteers, and participants. It can send a press release to hundreds of media outlets in a second, and it can allow your entire staff to communicate instantly with each other no matter where they are.

Whatever the job or task, some form of technology can probably help you do it more efficiently and effectively. Your challenge is to adopt the right technology at the right time in the correct manner so you can take advantage of its leverage without straining human resources and draining financial resources.

It's a fine balance, and it's ongoing, but if you want to be a gold standard nonprofit, you must embrace technology, and the earlier you do it the better. Otherwise, the benefits of technology and all your competitors will pass you by—byte by byte.

Eleven questions to ask before making any technology purchase

1. What should we buy?
2. Why should we buy it?
3. When should we buy it?
4. How much money should we spend?
5. Who will install it?
6. Who will use it?
7. How much training is involved?
8. How will we manage and maintain it?
9. What impact or benefit will it have?
10. What is the real cost—short and long-term?
11. What types of disruption will it cause during the adoption process?

CHAPTER 13

Branding

Making yourself memorable

Reflect for a moment. When you hear the name "Tiger Woods," what's the first thing that comes to mind? Amazing golfer. Nike. Big smile. Focused. Unfaithful.

What comes to mind when you think about "Special Olympics"? Fun. Down syndrome. Disabilities. Great cause. Courage. Hope. Volunteers. How about when you hear these names? iPhone. American Idol. The Nature Conservancy. Twin Towers. Hillary Clinton. Donald Trump. Wal-Mart. Statue of Liberty. Mercedes Benz. Harley Davidson. Kleenex.

Each of these names is a powerful brand. What is a brand? A brand is an image, impression, idea, or belief formed and *held* in a person's mind. In the case of Tiger Woods, his brand is the sum total of images, impressions, ideas, and beliefs held by everyone that knows him. The same is true for all the names listed above.

Why is branding important?

Branding is a *First Things First* principle because the public's image of your nonprofit is wrapped up in your brand. A good image can contribute significantly to your nonprofit's ability to fulfill its mission, and a bad image can harm it.

In fact, your image (brand) alone can make or break your success. This is why it's very important to build a strong, positive brand from the day you open for business. You want to explode out of the gate with credibility, integrity, and a positive magnetism that attracts widespread support.

You also want to build a strong brand early on because brands create interest that can become contagious. If people hold strong, positive beliefs and images about your nonprofit and mission, they will be eager and willing to share their experiences and impressions. This will inspire others to learn more and get involved, and then they will share their experiences and impressions.

You cannot start this spiral of brand momentum early enough. If you do it wisely, door upon door of opportunity will swing open wide.

Just because a brand is well-known doesn't mean it's strong and effective. Think of the names General Electric and Proctor & Gamble. What do they do? Most likely you think of them as big companies that make a lot of valuable things that touch our daily lives. But what are they *best* known for? That's a little more difficult to answer, isn't it? If you try to be everything to everybody, you may wind up with a weak brand.

The Salvation Army is another widely known brand. Other than ringing bells to collect money at Christmas, name three other things they do? Actually, they do a lot. They give millions away each year to support initiatives that locate missing persons, run camps for underprivileged youth, feed the elderly, rehabilitate prison inmates, promote drug and alcohol prevention, provide safe havens for victims of human trafficking, and much more.

Why don't people know more about the good work the Salvation Army does? People don't know because the Salvation Army does a poor job of promoting their brand. I can only imagine how much more money they could raise, and how many more people the Salvation Army could help, if they managed their brand more wisely.

The worst type of brand you can have is a negative brand. Negative brands are destructive. Remember the lead paint scare surrounding Christmas toys made in China? Years later, China's toy manufacturing industry is still reeling from the debacle. How about the *E. coli* scare that swarmed fast food icon, Jack in the Box? And what about Bernie Madoff; how would you like to have his brand?

Board drama, disgruntled employees, executive corruption, injured participants, or any negligent act has the potential to damage a brand and potentially destroy, or seriously impact, a nonprofit. It can take years, even decades, to restore a damaged brand. If a nonprofit is lucky enough to restore its image, it's likely the brand will forever remain weak with lingering fragments of negative impressions or stigmas.

As a nonprofit leader, you need to realize the importance of building and managing a strong, positive brand while avoiding situations and events that can harm or taint it. Your brand will reflect everything your nonprofit says, does, and believes, and it will be more powerful than all the money you raise or programming you develop. Your brand will be the sheen of the gold standard you hope to achieve and there is no better time to start buffing it than right now. First things first!

Case Study: Good ultimately prevails

Sun Valley Adaptive Sports was founded in 1999. The small nonprofit was a little known brand in a resort town of 25,000. Its first significant brand recognition came about in 2002 at a regional level when two of its participants, one a paraplegic and the other a leg amputee, became nationally ranked Paralympic alpine ski racers through its adaptive ski program.

In 2004, the SVAS brand experienced a blip of national fame when it became one of the first adaptive sports organizations to provide sports and recreation therapy for men and women of the armed forces who had been severely wounded in Iraq and Afghanistan.

SVAS had a timely and meaningful mission—two useful attributes for building a strong brand in the nonprofit world. They ran highly visible, year-round outdoor programs serving children, teens, adults, and veterans with disabilities. This gave people in the community many hands-on volunteer opportunities to connect with SVAS participants, or to observe SVAS programming taking place at a variety of public venues.

Citizens could watch blind veterans learn to ski on the same ski runs where they skied, teach children with autism how to swim at the YMCA where they swam, and see adults with Down syndrome enjoying community concerts they attended.

The SVAS brand was on the verge of explosive growth in the summer of 2005, when a series of public incidents brought six years of brand goodwill to a screeching halt. If you haven't guessed already, I'm referring to the blowout that took place when the SVAS founder threw his office keys at the board chair on Main Street and shouted, "I quit!"

This event, and the drama and dogfighting that followed, show how a single event in the life of a nonprofit can have a devastating ripple effect. Make sure your board and staff take preventative measures to avoid such blunders and manage the fallout quickly and wisely when they do happen.

Now, having a founder or chief executive quit isn't always cause for alarm. Although in the case of SVAS, it was catastrophic. Following the Main Street shootout, a slew of email wars began between the founder, board members, and staff. The founder was blaming the board for all that had gone wrong and the board was blaming the founder.

Like most contentious breakups, it was all about who was "right" and who was "wrong." Hackles raised, fingers pointed, and rumors flew. Pride and stubbornness stood tall like battleground flags. Both sides dug deep emotional trenches and the mudslinging fiasco that unfolded rivaled the vilest political smear campaigns.

In a small town, news and gossip travel quickly. Everyone wanted to know if the board had treated the founder unfairly and forced the founder to resign. Or, was the founder having difficulty fulfilling his job responsibilities and quit out of frustration?

The community wanted answers and clarity. What they got instead was a slurry of confusing information and changing stories. Donors cast their votes by closing their checkbooks. Premier business partners sat on the sidelines. SVAS operations disintegrated. The volunteer base dwindled, key staff resigned, and the program coordinator wallowed in tears. It was a mess.

In a small town, this type of drama is big news. One of the local papers decided to do some investigative reporting. The goal was to uncover facts and provide context. The resulting article was tepid and did little to change public opinion. The reporter even admitted she was baffled by the escapade—too many stories, too many powerful emotions, and too many big egos.

The ordeal eventually created what amounted to a Continental Divide in the community. People loyal to the founder believed his story. People loyal to the board believed the board's story.

I was hired during the height of the chaos, and the board's top priority for me was to manage SVAS' public relations nightmare and restore the brand. Lucky me, huh?

With no time to waste, I established three objectives: Stop the board and staff from talking—and gossiping—about the founder and the incidents that surrounded his departure; rebuild every operational and programmatic structure with an emphasis on quality; and create a massive wave of compelling stories to share with the media about our good work and noble mission.

The board and staff approved the strategy. Once the objectives were underway, everyone was relieved because the endless bickering had done nothing but drain resources from programming, taint the brand, and fuel anger from the founder.

Opting to take the "high road" proved to be a wise decision, but it was a test of patience and perseverance as the board and staff had to deal with a two-year onslaught of jabs and criticisms from a founder reluctant to accept a truce.

On the practical side of things, the staff immediately kicked off its plan to restructure programming and operations, and restore the SVAS brand. In a swift and unanimous decision, we decided it would be better to scrap everything and rebuild the organization from the ground up, rather than try to fix creaky floorboards and put a fresh coat of paint on a house that was built on a crumbling foundation.

The board agreed. The next morning, we brought in our wrecking balls and bulldozers and leveled six years of low-performance programming, outdated policies and procedures, shoddy business practices, and antiquated technology.

Staff worked seven days a week around the clock to restructure every functional area of the organization. We wrote operational plans, designed new collateral material, and built a new website. We retooled the mission, established a set of core values, rewrote our bylaws, and created dozens of first-time governance policies.

We didn't stop there. We created new brand identities for every program, launched a volunteer program, and established job descriptions for staff. I think the only thing we kept from the previous administration was the name of the nonprofit (Sun Valley Adaptive Sports)—and we thought about changing that too!

We rebuilt the foundation of SVAS in 60 days. We then set our sights on becoming a national model for adaptive sports therapy by creating gold standard programming, sustainable funding, efficient and effective operations, and a respected brand of national prominence.

Creating a respected brand turned out to be the most difficult task because our brand was starting from such a weak and mostly negative position. To reverse the polarity, we made it a goal to do whatever it took to secure some type of positive media exposure every week about the good work we were doing.

We worked hard running innovative programs that transformed people's lives and then worked just as hard to share these stories in a compelling manner. We wrote press releases for every major success and accomplishment. Staff made dozens of radio and television appearances and gave dozens more newspaper and magazine interviews. I gave talks at the American Legion, Rotary, and local chamber of commerce functions.

Local media exposure led to regional exposure that quickly led to national exposure. I was soon doing interviews with talk show hosts on national television and radio, giving speeches at the Pentagon, and participating in roundtable conferences to establish the strategic direction of the adaptive sports industry.

In two years, we had secured more than 150 "exposures" in major media including Newsweek, ABC Nightline, and CNN. The more media we received, the more calls we received. The phone rang almost weekly from media giants such as TIME, U.S. News, Fox News, LA Times, and the Huffington Post.

I was most blown away when companies such as Explore and Fox News (Lieutenant Colonel Oliver North's film team) began calling us to produce short films and documentaries about the therapeutic work we were doing for wounded veterans. We also received calls from award-winning independent filmmakers offering their videography services for free.

SVAS was a brand builder's dream come true. It all seems so distant now, but we had transformed a collapsing nonprofit and a dying brand into a gold standard nonprofit with widespread brand recognition.

It took two years, but the mudslinging residue between the founder and board eventually faded. Good ultimately prevails. As we had hoped, the massive wave of compelling stories of our good work had washed away the drama and helped restore our brand.

Our new challenge was managing our success. We were growing at a rate of 100 percent a year. By 2009, we were managing hundreds of donors and volunteers, and we were fielding calls from dozens of organizations around the country asking for advice on how to run a program like ours.

Money was pouring in at an average rate of $200,000 a month and we began exploring ways to raise $30 million to build the nation's largest nonmedical rehabilitation center for wounded veterans! It was all a bit crazy and outrageous, and the thrilling ride continues today thanks to a focused effort to build gold standard programming and a strong, positive brand.

You want to build a strong brand early on so you can take advantage of the leverage and impact a strong brand provides. It's easy to get lost in the dozens of things you *could* do to build and manage your brand, but here are some simple tactics you *should* do.

Tactics and Tips
Take inventory: How does your brand rate?
The first thing you need to do when building or reshaping a brand is to find out what people *really* think about your programming, operations, mission, staff, and board. You'll also want to find out what images, beliefs, and opinions people hold.

The fastest way to do this is to put together a simple, anonymous survey of 10-15 questions and give it to 25 people willing to answer the questions candidly and objectively. Respondents should be a mix of people who are familiar and unfamiliar with your nonprofit.

A good list would include a small number of people from each of these categories: donors, volunteers, business partners, reporters, participants, family members of participants, and local residents. Frame questions in a manner that encourages people to share honest thoughts and feelings.

Here are some examples: "What image comes to mind when you think of our organization?" "How would you explain our reputation in the community?" "What word comes to mind when you think of our chief executive?" "In one sentence, how would you describe our staff?"

Here are some more examples: "What brief statement best describes the quality of our services?" "In three words or less, what image or impression comes to mind when you think of our board, staff, programming, mission, workplace, equipment, public outreach, and community impact?" "What could we do to inspire you to volunteer?" "What phrase would you use to describe the benefit we provide our clients?"

If you're a startup nonprofit, you'll want to frame your questions to address the future. For example: "How would you feel if Pam Smith, a long-time resident of the community, became our executive director?" "How do you think people in the community would feel if we started an adaptive sports program for people with disabilities?" "What comes to mind when you hear our name?" "What do you like and dislike about our name?" "When you see our logo, what impression does it make on you?" "What response does our tagline elicit when you read it?"

You get the picture. The goal is to ask a handful of probing questions to unveil what the public thinks about your nonprofit and what images, impressions, and beliefs they hold in their hearts and minds. The results are usually startling and often humbling. Most importantly, the exercise provides a starting point for building a brand.

Define your brand
Once you've taken inventory of your brand, you'll need to define your brand. This is often an elaborate and time-consuming process because the details of defining a brand can be complex.

To simplify the process, and save you a lot of time, I'm going to suggest you focus on the most important facets of defining your brand. Once these are in place, you can refine your brand as resources permit.

To start the process, write brief answers to the following questions:

1. What services do we offer? Define the qualities of these services.
2. What is our mission? Or, what is our purpose for being in business?
3. What are the core values that best define our nonprofit?
4. What differentiates us as a nonprofit?
5. Who or what benefits from our services?
6. How does our nonprofit benefit the community?
7. What is our tagline? What does it say about us?

Using your answers from questions 1-7, create a *one-page* personality or character profile for your nonprofit centered on your primary reason for existing and the primary services you offer. Think of the profile as a short biography or long personal ad. Take this exercise seriously. Write it so well, and with such creativity and conviction, that it would motivate donors to support you after reading it.

This is also the point where you'll want to refer to the feedback you received from your survey. If you discover *major* differences between the images, impressions, and beliefs you hope to create in people's minds and the actual images, impressions, and beliefs you have created, you'll need to find ways to reconcile these differences.

If you decide to appeal to the *existing* images, impressions, and beliefs currently held by people, then change your profile. This may require you to make adjustments to programming and operations. If you want to *change* people's images, impressions, and beliefs of your nonprofit, you'll have to use various marketing techniques to make these changes (see next section). This too may require you to make changes to programming and operations.

Unfortunately, the branding tactics you'll need to employ to reconcile major differences are beyond the scope of this book. If you find yourself in this position, consult a professional brand manager; he can help you develop strategies to work through this complicated challenge.

Once you've completed the profile, you'll need to whittle it down to the *essence* of who you are and what images, impressions, and beliefs you want people to hold in their minds when they think about your nonprofit. If you've done a good job of building your core values, mission statement, and statement of purpose, then much of the time-consuming work is done. Your task now is to articulate your essence in one or two sentences.

As you go through the refining process, you'll quickly see how easy it would be to establish various brands for all aspects of your nonprofit: staff, board, volunteers, operations, and every program and service offered. These are things you can do later as you refine your brand. What you need to do *first* is establish a core brand for your entire nonprofit, one that contains the *essential* images, impressions, and beliefs you want people to hold in their minds.

In Sun Valley, our participants, our community, and the leaders in the industries we served held many positive images and impressions about SVAS. But when boiled down, the essence of who we were, what we did, and what we stood for could be stated as, "Gold standard adaptive sports programming." This was our brand. It's what we delivered, it's what we wanted people to think, and it's what people believed.

If I had to write a more descriptive version of our brand it would read something like, "An innovative adaptive sports organization with gold standard programming that makes lasting and meaningful change in the lives of people with disabilities."

Before you can build or promote a brand, you must first clearly define the core images and impressions you want to hold in people's minds. What word or phrase would be the essence of what you want people to think about when they think of your nonprofit?

Fine-tune the marketing mix

After defining your core brand, you'll want to call on a variety of marketing functions to build, enhance, and sustain your brand. This will include publicity, public relations, promotion, and advertising. Your goal is to develop an effective and affordable mix of marketing functions to accomplish your brand building objectives.

You'll also need to make decisions about the best time to promote a program, the most effective combination of media to use when launching an advertising campaign, the most effective tone and style to use when writing an annual report, and the most important points to cover in a fundraising speech. Every major business function that connects your nonprofit to the public will likely include some marketing component. The combination of all your marketing efforts is your *marketing mix*.

I'm sure you can see how the task of developing a marketing mix could get complicated very quickly. This is why you need to have a professional understanding of how to use marketing functions to inform and persuade others about all the great work you're doing. If you don't, you'll wind up with a wimpy brand that falls far short of its potential.

~ ~ ~

Get a marketing guru on your team

If you're a small nonprofit, it's doubtful you have the funds to hire a marketing director. You probably don't even have the funds to outsource the work to a marketing consultant. So, what do you do?

Hopefully, your chief executive, or one of your key staff, has a professional understanding of marketing and branding. This is the best solution for many nonprofits. If you hired a high quality social entrepreneur as your chief executive, you'll be in good shape, because most are master marketers and brand builders.

If not, find out if any of your board members or volunteers have professional-level marketing skills and experience. If someone is gracious enough to help—perfect! However, take time to determine if they are qualified. I've learned the best intentions of the kindest volunteers can result in shoddy work that costs thousands of dollars to undo or redo.

A great place to find marketing talent is at a local publicity, public relations, or communications firm. Many are willing to provide pro bono or discounted advice and services to nonprofits.

Mid-sized to large-sized corporations are also possibilities. They usually have one or two talented in-house marketing staff willing to do in-kind work to help local nonprofits.

As soon as you can afford it, hire a master marketer. Until then, as soon as you can, find someone with professional-level knowledge and experience willing to take the helm of your marketing and branding efforts.

Use the media to strengthen and promote your brand

Suppose you had a dream of opening an animal shelter. You scrimped and saved for 15 years, and for the last six months, you've worked day and night painting walls, building cages, and training volunteers.

A week before you open, you call the local paper and ask if they'd be willing to send a reporter to cover the ribbon-cutting event. They happily oblige.

When Sunday's paper hits the stands, you see your daughter on the front page of the "Local Vibe" section with a warm smile and an armful of golden retriever puppies. The feature tells a compelling story of how you spent your childhood rescuing injured birds and stray kittens and why you gave up a high-paying corporate job to live a quiet life in a small town to fulfill your dream of running an animal shelter.

For the next few weeks, people you've never seen come up to you in the grocery store, bank, and coffee shop to thank you for your charitable efforts and wish you good luck. You find your mailbox lined with donations and you receive calls and emails from people wanting to know how they can volunteer.

Over the next year, you're so busy running programs and raising money that you neglect to do any marketing. Deep down, you believe marketing is an unnecessary expense and think, "Why spend the time and money to create a video, promote our work on social media, or produce a nice looking annual report; I'd rather spend it on animal care."

Soon, donations begin to slip. Volunteer hours drop in half. Reporters no longer call. At the same time, you notice other nonprofits getting frequent attention in the newspaper, on television, and on the radio. There is a lot of buzz around town about them and little about you. This hurts and you feel a little jealous. You believe you deserve as much attention as the next nonprofit.

You're not really sure what to do. You're worried and stressed, and with each passing month donations decline, eventually forcing you to make cutbacks in services and staff. Your dream of rescuing injured critters is now a problem of survival.

Get noticed and get personal
This story is not uncommon. Media coverage is favorable when a nonprofit first opens because it's *newsworthy*. The result is a spike in community awareness, donations, and volunteers. If a nonprofit fails to sustain the public's interest, it won't take long before support and funding begin to fade.

Your goal is to make yourself a fluorescent, flashing dot in the middle of the media's radar screen. One way to do this is to create a steady stream of stories and events so compelling and newsworthy, reporters and producers feel obligated to cover them for fear a competitor may get the story first.

Creating compelling, newsworthy stories and events will get you plenty of media coverage, but if you want regular front-page features and primetime coverage, you need to establish personal relationships with writers, reporters, anchors, editors, and producers who create and produce the articles and shows.

I covered this topic in Chapter Nine, but it's worth repeating because the impact of quality media coverage is invaluable to a nonprofit. A cover story can inspire a new donor to support your mission who then goes on to become your biggest donor. A feature segment on a nationally syndicated cable show can provide immense credibility to your brand, and a powerful interview on a local television station can motivate new volunteers to sign up.

You may secure a few slots of media coverage by your own efforts, but if you want to secure *frequent* media coverage over a long period of time, you'll need to develop personal relationships with media personnel who have the power and influence to make things happen.

If you live in a small town, this task is fairly easy. The tactic here is to send compelling press releases and novel ideas for stories because local publishers and producers have an insatiable appetite for the new and unusual to capture and hold the attention of their readers and viewers. They crave quality work because so many of the local press releases and stories they receive look as if they had been written and laid out by a tenth grader.

You'll also want to make time to get to know reporters and producers personally by taking them out for a cup of coffee now and then, and always writing thank-you cards and notes of appreciation after receiving any type of media coverage. You'll find personnel at local media respond strongly to the personal touch.

If you live in a larger town, grabbing media attention is more difficult, but not impossible. Big city reporters and producers often insulate themselves from the public. They have hundreds of businesses and nonprofits clawing at them for attention, so you'll need to work harder to get a meeting, and even harder to get them out of the office.

Big cities typically have community-based newspapers, magazines, radio stations, cable shows, podcasts, and websites. If you're willing to make the effort, you'll find reporters and producers of these niche media outlets just as accessible as those in small towns. Once you establish a personal relationship with them, their eyes and ears will open a little wider when you submit a press release or suggest they cover an event you're hosting.

The media is one of the most powerful and cost-effective tools you can use to build your brand, enhance your credibility, and sustain community interest in your mission. Make a commitment to create the most compelling stories you can, as often as you can, and develop *personal* relationships with those in the media who have the power and influence to make big things happen.

Help the media help you

If you want to win favor and make friends with the media, help them do their jobs. For example, if a local magazine calls to interview you for a feature story about your new program, send the writer a package of collateral material, press releases, video clips, a list of interview questions, and links to any other pertinent support material about the program and your nonprofit.

Send the package one week prior to the interview. This way the writer has a chance to formulate a vision for the feature and the types of questions he needs to ask during the interview. The day of the interview, come prepared. Bring a copy of the press release, support collateral, interview questions, and a set of high quality photos copied to a thumb drive. Once the interview begins, remember to smile, breathe, and let your passion shine bright in all you say and do.

Here's another tactic you can use to help the media and secure media placement: send a reporter a compelling, high-resolution photo of something your nonprofit accomplished. It could be a young child receiving her first ribbon, a family receiving a food basket, or a paraplegic skiing for the first time. The photo must elicit a strong emotional response. In fact, the more "wow" factor a photo exhibits, the better. The media loves wow.

You'll want to write a catchy header and a concise caption for the photo. If you have time, include a short sidebar of information to provide additional context. Keep the sidebar to 75 words or less and write concise and captivating sentences.

Editors, reporters, and bloggers crave these types of submissions because most of the work is done before it reaches their desks; all they need to do is tweak a word or two, resize the photo and they're good to go. Many times, if it's well written and laid out nicely, they'll run the entire submission unedited.

You can also help the media by offering to set up and take down their props, hold interviews at their offices instead of yours to reduce their travel burden, and offer to help organize and subsidize flights, lodging, and meals to encourage national media to visit.

Building relationships with media personnel takes time and effort. You're busy enough doing your job, so why should you help the media do theirs? Because most nonprofits don't make the effort to help, which is why they don't get media coverage and why their brands melt away and their funding dries up.

You're different. The media likes different. If you want a strong and credible brand, you must have the media talking and writing about what you're doing as often as possible. One of the best ways to do this, and one of the best ways to win their hearts in the process, is to help the media do their jobs.

Craft consistent and compelling messages
The majority of people don't really know what their favorite nonprofit does or where it's headed because the messages of many nonprofits are unclear, inconsistent, or nonexistent.

If your staff, board, and volunteers are unclear about what your nonprofit does and where it's going, then the public will be unclear. If the public is unclear, your brand will be weak and so will your ability to raise money and rally supporters to sustain your nonprofit.

When building a brand, you want to craft and communicate messages about your programs, services, and operations that are consistent, compelling, powerful, and memorable. These messages should come through loud and clear in all you say and do. This means talking about them at board meetings and volunteer training sessions, placing them in collateral material and on websites, and sharing them with donors and the media.

Always be thinking of new and better ways to construct messages that create images, mold impressions, and influence behavior. Look for ways to write dramatic personal achievement stories, share testimonials, show emotional photos, or create memorable slogans such as Nike's "Just do it!" or The Nature Conservancy's "Preserving nature, protecting life."

Sometimes you'll want to use messages to inform and other times you'll want to use messages to educate or entertain. No matter what your intention, always, always think about what message is best suited to influence a particular audience and make a lasting impression. Words and messages are powerful tools to build and sustain a brand—choose them wisely and place them carefully.

Spread a virus

Do you remember when bookstores restricted the release of Harry Potter books? By restricting supply, they created a panic of demand. TV crews around the world showed up at bookstores to film boys and girls camping out for days on sidewalks as they anxiously awaited the arrival of the latest adventure of Harry and his Hogwarts cronies. Supplies quickly ran dry, creating more demand and tens of millions in sales. Toys-R-Us and Apple employed similar tactics during the release of Tickle-Me-Elmo dolls and iPhones.

The marketing tactic of restricting supply to create demand is a facet of a broader marketing technique called *viral marketing*. In its simplest form, viral marketing compels people to share their thoughts, feelings, and information about a product, service, idea, or business with other people. Viral marketing is a clever branding tactic, and the bigger the buzz you can create, the better. Used effectively, especially on the Internet, it can be a potent force to create, strengthen, or broaden a brand.

I used viral marketing a number of times at SVAS to broaden our brand. I once talked with a local reporter and intentionally leaked news about our desire to open the nation's largest nonmedical rehabilitation center for wounded veterans with traumatic brain injuries and post-traumatic stress disorder.

If you recall, we received an offer to buy a local boutique hotel for $10 million. Our vision was to buy it and then convert it into a rehabilitation center. I thought, "What better way to draw attention to the vision for the center than to quietly leak a few details about our intentions, rather than blurting out all the details in a press release." The tactic was sublime. The following day, the reporter wrote a one-paragraph blurb under a bold headline on the front page of the local paper that read, "Rehabilitation center for wounded veterans may open!"

This created a wildfire of buzz and chatter around town because the center, if opened, would rekindle the town's legacy of helping wounded veterans dating back to WWII, when the Sun Valley resort was transformed into a naval convalescent hospital and served more than 7,000 men and women of the armed forces who had been severely wounded in the battles of Iwo Jima and Okinawa.

Many community leaders thought the center would help boost tourism, create jobs, and convey a positive image to the nation that Sun Valley was a "patriotic community, committed to giving back." Others felt the center and the majestic surroundings would make lasting impressions on the wounded veterans: "Sun Valley . . . the place that changed my life!" Both messages would provide powerful impressions to strengthen the community's image and brand.

Within two weeks, it seemed like everyone in town and in our industry was talking about the center. "When will the center be open?" "How big will it be?" "How many jobs will it create?" "How many wounded veterans will it help?" "What type of rehabilitation services will it offer?" "Will the government help fund it?"

As news of the center spread, calls flooded in. Newspapers, magazines and television stations from around the country called for interviews. A new wave of foundations and donors called saying they would like to help fund the center. Therapists and nurses called from as far away as New Zealand wanting to move to Sun Valley and work at the center—some for free.

In four months, we raised $3.5 million in pledges, received 42 different types of media coverage, and signed up 23 new volunteers. Though we were unable to raise the $10 million to buy the hotel within the timeframe established in the purchase agreement, the impact on SVAS remained an unexpected blessing that astonished us all.

This example shows how a single piece of compelling news can perpetuate a brand in unimaginable ways. I'll admit, I purposely started the so-called leak to stimulate interest and curiosity about our wounded veteran program and the rehabilitation center. But I had no idea it would lend so much credibility to our brand and lead to millions of dollars in funding—and it all started by sharing a one-sentence message to a reporter at a wine bar.

If you want to raise money, sustain your mission, and keep your programs front and center in everyone's mind, find ways to get people talking about your nonprofit in a manner that compels them to tell their family, friends, and everyone they know.

Recognize everyone is a brand

Some Japanese companies don't have marketing departments because they believe everyone is responsible for marketing. To them, every act is a marketing act, every employee is a brand. And The Four Seasons doesn't hire anyone with hotel experience, except senior management. Instead, they have a training culture centered on great customer service and "brand experience."

Nonprofits of all sizes can learn a snippet of sage advice from these marketing philosophies. If the objective of building a brand is to create and sustain images and impressions in the minds of people, then it makes smart business sense to have as many people as possible communicating your brand messages through their words and actions.

Are your volunteers so thrilled with the work they're doing that they share their experiences every chance they get? Are your board members so excited about their involvement that they ask their best friends to join the board? Is it obvious to the public that your staff lives and breathes your core values? Are your donors so impressed with the impact you're making that they tell their friends to support you?

Creating meaningful experiences for people connected with your nonprofit is a surefire way to inspire people to share their experiences.

You'll also want to inspire people to share specific messages about your nonprofit. The messages should be simple and memorable. Your volunteer coordinator can share your mission statement at training sessions. Your chief executive can remind board members of your core values at board meetings. You can design newspaper ads to highlight catch phrases about the work you do and the vision you have.

Every person connected with your nonprofit is a potential brand ambassador. It's your job to provide emotional experiences and powerful messages that inspire people to tell everyone they know about what you do and why they should get involved.

Advertise – It's an investment

Most nonprofits view advertising as an expense. "We shouldn't be advertising; if we spend money on anything, it should be on programs." "Donors will think we're squandering their money if we advertise." "We're too busy as it is; we can't afford to be spending time building ads." "What value does advertising provide anyway?"

This is old-school thinking. Smart nonprofits view advertising as an investment and use the power of advertising to reinforce brand messages and images. You should do the same. Once you establish a brand, advertise in specific media channels to specific audiences to reinforce specific messages and images. This means you want to use advertising as a tool to *support* your brand, rather than a tool to *create* your brand.

At SVAS, I used to run a half-page ad in our local paper every three months. In large type, the ad listed the names of businesses and people who contributed to our most recent wounded veteran sports camps. The ad also showed touching, powerful photos of wounded veterans learning different types of sports for the first time.

Below the photos ran text thanking the contributors for their support, followed by our tagline, "Higher Ground . . . Healing America's Wounded Veterans!"

The purpose of the ads was not to raise money or solicit volunteers—though they did. The purpose of the ads was to *remind* people in the community of the noble and patriotic work we were doing by showing compelling photos of our programming and thanking those who had contributed to make it happen.

We wanted people to see the ads and think, "Oh, yeah, Sun Valley Adaptive Sports . . . that's the wonderful nonprofit doing amazing work to rehabilitate wounded soldiers returning from Iraq . . . how wonderful . . . thanks so much for reminding me."

Running reminder ads like the ones we ran can help you keep important images and messages (your brand) front and center in the minds of your supporters. This is important when it comes time to ask for donations and solicit volunteers because people will be mentally and emotionally prepped and more likely to respond.

You can achieve similar results by running 30-second radio spots and 60-second television spots as part of your local and regional "reminder" advertising campaign. Website advertising can be effective if targeted. National publications and cable channels can reach larger audiences, but they are costly.

A well-designed ad placed in any type of media can generate buzz and attention that eventually leads to new volunteers, surprise donations, or deepened business relationships. You just never know.

Leave the details of advertising design and placement to your marketing guru. Your responsibility is to view advertising as an investment to support your brand. Include it in your marketing strategy and budget funds to pay for it.

Differentiate and build credibility

Branding means ownership. If you want to create a powerful and memorable brand, you'll need to *own* images, impressions, or beliefs in the minds of people connected to your nonprofit, or people you want to connect to your nonprofit.

One of the best ways to create this type of ownership is being the first at something, the best at something, or the best known for something. This might be a program or service you offer, a type of client you serve, the quality of your programming, the type of change you make in the lives of your clients, the type of research you conduct, or the impact you've made in the community.

At SVAS, we made an effort to own a number of images and impressions. For our volunteers, it was "SVAS is a fun and professional place to help people with disabilities and give back to wounded veterans." For our industry: "SVAS offers the most innovative and therapeutic adaptive sports programming in the nation to rehabilitate wounded veterans." For our donors: "SVAS is the best social investment I can make with the money I donate." For the community: "SVAS does meaningful work for people with disabilities and provides tremendous value to the community."

What is your nonprofit best known for? What do you do better than anyone else? What would you like to do better than anyone else? How can you differentiate yourself? When volunteers hear the name of your nonprofit, what do you want them to think? What about donors? Business partners? Industry leaders? The community?

Being a leader in a particular area is a strong motivating factor to influence behavior. It also builds a tremendous amount of credibility, and credibility helps widen the appeal of a brand. You should strive to attain a leadership position in your industry and in your community.

This will require an exceptional amount of hard work, because to attain and sustain a leadership position, you'll have to uphold the highest standards of performance and excellence in all aspects of programming and operations. If you can achieve these lofty objectives, you're sure to experience an avalanche of support and attention.

You're learning that there are many things you can do to build and promote a strong, positive brand. No matter what combination of tactics you use, be sure to put the tactic of differentiation near the top of your list. It's one of the most effective branding tactics a nonprofit can use when limited resources and tight budgets prevail.

Choose a meaningful name and logo
The name you choose for your nonprofit plays a significant role in your branding strategy. Over time, people will associate your name with what you do.

Mention of your name or the sight of your logo will elicit various images, messages, thoughts, and feelings. If your name or logo is confusing, difficult to remember, or difficult to pronounce, you run the risk of weakening your brand and losing supporters.

How about this name: "CPRRWLRNA." Yep, it's a real name. Okay, it's an acronym for a name, but still, what kind of acronym has nine letters and doesn't even sound like a common word?

The acronym stands for Conservation Professionals for the Restoration and Reclamation of Wilderness Land and Rivers in North America. This may be a terrific organization; I don't know. But I do know the founding members understand tree bark and salmon better than they understand marketing and branding.

When you choose a name for your nonprofit, select one that is simple, understandable, and rolls off the tongue easily. For example, "The Red Cross," "Feeding America," and "Reno Botanical Society."

If the name can convey your mission or a service you provide, so much the better. "The Nature Conservancy," "Rady Children's Hospital," and "CARE" (Cooperative for Assistance and Relief Everywhere).

Your logo and taglines should also be simple and understandable. Again, it's okay to be edgy and artistic, but not at the cost of being confusing or bizarre. Logos should use simple graphics without clutter. This is important because you may want to reduce the size of a logo to make pins or enlarge it to make banners. Use font styles that are legible and scalable.

It's also important to use colors that reflect the culture of what you do. For example, if you ran a nonprofit similar to The Nature Conservancy, you wouldn't want to use the color red for a logo if your intention is to convey a feeling of serenity and tranquility. Red conveys energy, war, danger, power, passion, love, and strength. It would be more effective to use soothing and joyful earth tone colors such as green, yellow, blue, maple, and light brown.

Some nonprofits have one logo, but many taglines. Different taglines allow you to reinforce different messages depending on the audience you're targeting, or the marketing tactic you're using. In the case of our Higher Ground program, we decided the primary tagline should elicit a positive, emotional, and patriotic response with donors:

"Higher Ground: Healing America's Wounded Veterans"

However, when communicating with wounded veterans who attended our program, we wanted to avoid labeling them as "wounded." So, in the literature we sent them and the gift clothing we embroidered for them, we used the tagline:

"Higher Ground: New Heights, New Horizons"

Your name, logo, and taglines will become synonymous with your brand, so spend time early on to make wise decisions about how people will perceive them, now and in the future.

Takeaways

Everything your nonprofit says and does creates images and impressions in people's minds. These people share their images and impressions with other people. These impressions, one by one, either build or dilute your brand and have a direct impact on your success.

Most young nonprofits know very little about marketing and branding. They say they need a brochure, but they're not sure what to include in it to make it effective. Even if they know they should include stories and photos, they typically don't know how to write *compelling* stories or take *gripping* photos—techniques that make powerful impact. They say they want a strong brand, but the truth is they're not really sure how to go about creating one.

You can leapfrog the competition, inspire people to join your cause, change public perception, raise bundles of money, and fulfill your mission if you understand and apply razor sharp marketing and branding tactics. Funders and supporters are seeking reliable experiences with desired outcomes. Your brand is a key asset in the process of shaping and meeting these expectations.

Start by finding someone who will offer professional marketing advice for free or at a nominal fee. Create a simple and understandable name and logo. Design powerful messages and images. Differentiate yourself. Build credibility by harnessing the power of the media and becoming a leader in your industry and in your community. Fine-tune an effective mix of marketing tactics. Get people talking about your nonprofit by creating a virus. Make friends with the media and help people working in the industry do their jobs. Get published. Get on TV. Advertise.

To some, branding is complicated and confusing, and to others it's smoke and mirrors. But the most successful nonprofits, the ones raising big money and grabbing the most media coverage, know that creating a strong, positive, and recognizable brand represents enduring value and is one of the most powerful tools of leverage a nonprofit can possess.

Don't delay. Start building a winning brand strategy today—you could even start by leaking a story or two.

CHAPTER 14

One-on-One Fundraising
Raising big money in personal settings

P eople buy things from people they like and trust. You buy your morning latte at Cam's Coffee Cabin because Cam greets you by name when you walk in and knows exactly how you like your latte made. You shop at a family owned drugstore because you trust the friendly and helpful staff. You buy produce at a roadside farmer's stand because you know the farmer.

The same principle applies to raising money. Whether it's a major donor, grants manager, or CEO of a large corporation, your chances of getting funded increase tenfold if you have a healthy, *personal* relationship with the potential contributor and you can meet him or her in person to make an appeal.

The Harvard Business Review once published an article on the most effective methods of communication that lead to giving. Here's a ranked list along with a couple of additions I gleaned from similar studies:

1. One-on-one meetings
2. Small group meetings or parties
3. Telephone conversations
4. Personalized handwritten letters
5. Personalized typed letters
6. Email or text solicitation (those with videos and pics did better)
7. Web, blog, video, and other online solicitation
8. Galas or large group events
9. Direct mail with no personalization that included a video
10. Direct mail with no personalization
11. Grants
12. Brochure distribution
13. Advertisements

Notice the two most effective methods center on talking with people in small, intimate settings. I suspect you thought "annual fundraisers" would rank higher, but this tactic didn't even make the top half. Another surprise might be advertising. Some nonprofits use advertising to raise money, but as you can see, it ranks last. In fact, fundraising ads in local newspapers yield a meager response rate of .05 percent or less.

However, as you learned in the last chapter, advertising is an excellent marketing tactic to *support* a brand, which can eventually lead to funding. So, as a footnote, don't discount the power of advertising because it's ranked last here. Just be sure to use advertising to do what it does best.

The response rate to direct mail pieces isn't much better than advertising; it averages 3.0 percent. The response rate of canvassing or cold calling new prospects is 10 percent. But if a person making an appeal knows the donor, the response rate can be as high as 50 percent. If a person making an appeal has a long-term, healthy and personal relationship with the donor, and meets with the donor in a one-on-one or small group setting, the response rate can exceed 80 percent!

Why is one-on-one fundraising important?

One-on-one fundraising is a *First Things First* principle because soliciting money in person is the most effective way to raise money—big money. Meeting donors in person gives them a chance to feel your passion, understand your work in detail, ask questions, establish trust, and connect with *you* personally, none of which can be effectively done through a brochure, proposal, bulk email, annual report, appeal letter, or website.

Funding is the fuel you need to build great programs, hire quality staff, and sustain a noble mission. As a leader of a nonprofit, no insight is more important to understand and apply to your fundraising efforts than this:

> More than 80 percent of all giving to nonprofits comes from individuals, and more than 80 percent of this money comes from one-on-one meetings, small group meetings and parties, and fundraisers.

What does this tell you? It tells you the winning formula to maximize the return on your fundraising efforts is to spend a large percentage of your time and effort developing relationships and making appeals in personal settings!

Other fundraising tactics, such as those listed in the Harvard Business Review article, can be effective if skillfully employed, but many of these tactics work best for more mature nonprofits with widespread fundraising resources such as a large fundraising staff, hefty marketing and fundraising budgets, and extensive mailing lists.

Smaller nonprofits don't have these luxuries. Even if they did, it's still most effective to raise money in one-on-one and small group settings. Think about it. If you can raise 80 percent of your money through three fundraising tactics, two of which rank as the top two most effective tactics, why not spend more time doing it? First things first!

Case Study: The cost of writing grants

On a snowy morning in December 2008, I received a letter from a foundation that made grants to nonprofits providing services to people with blindness. The letter noted one of the foundation's trustees had been skiing in Sun Valley a week earlier and saw some of our instructors teaching alpine skiing to wounded veterans who had lost their eyesight fighting in Iraq.

I called the foundation, talked with the director, and learned we fit their funding guidelines. "Great program!" she exclaimed. "We would like to help fund your next winter ski camp for blind veterans. How much does it cost to host a camp?"

I told her each weeklong ski camp costs $50,000 and covered everything from airfare to entertainment. "No, problem," she said casually. "I'll email a grant application today. Apply for $15,000. This will cover almost one-third of the costs of the camp."

We hung up the phone and I thought, "Well, that was easy." I then trotted over to the offices of my programming staff and shared the good news. A few days later, the application arrived. I thumbed through it and was floored by its length—40 pages, 167 questions.

Some grant applications are easy, some are difficult, but this was the grant application from hell. The application requested various graphs and information I had never been asked to produce in 20 years of grant writing. They even wanted to know if any of the staff had traveled out of the country recently. Really, I kid you not.

Our grant submission was 62 pages long and it took 60 hours to write. In January, we received a check for $15,000. With the check, came the grant acceptance letter. The letter stated the terms of the grant and indicated if we accepted the $15,000, we would be responsible to produce four quarterly reports and a year-end report. "Easy enough," I thought to myself, so I signed the letter and deposited the check.

Three months later, the foundation sent the first of the four reports we needed to complete. The grant application was a nightmare itself, but after reading the reporting requirements, my aggravation soared to new heights. The report was 25 pages long and I estimated it would take 30 hours to complete.

Working on the report was an exhaustive drain on my time and energy because I was the only one writing grants at the time and we were right in the middle of an expansion phase. I simply didn't have 30 hours to spare. Plus, it was overwhelming to think I had three more similar reports to complete as well as a year-end report.

At the time we received the grant, Sun Valley Adaptive Sports had 40 major donors, not including foundations, supporting our wounded veterans program. We defined a "major donor" as any donor that made a gift of $5,000 or more.

As chief executive, I was responsible for raising all (98 percent) of the funds to support SVAS and the Higher Ground program. Our board did a poor job of raising money, which put a lot of pressure on me to raise funds and manage donor relations, especially since we had no fundraising staff.

My circumstances left me no choice but to be as selective and efficient as possible in my efforts to raise funds. I made it my top priority to meet every major donor in a one-on-one setting for at least one hour once a year, twice if possible.

Whether we met for coffee, dinner, or for a few ski runs, my goal was to spend quality, personal time with donors to get to know them, develop a relationship, answer questions, and make appeals.

That year, I raised $935,000 during one-on-one meetings with major donors. Here's a quick breakdown: $370,000 from coffee and wine meetings, $75,000 from eight lunches, $100,000 from six ski outings, and $140,000 from four dinners. Most of the meetings ran an hour, though some of the dinners and outings ran two to four hours.

The largest gift resulted during a casual afternoon of fly fishing with a trustee of a major foundation. That resulted in a $250,000 gift—not bad when you consider our budget that year was $1.2 million.

I'm sure it comes as no surprise when I tell you the time and effort I put forth to attend lunch, dinner, wine, skiing, and fly fishing meetings was a lot more fun and raised a lot more money than the long and tedious task of spending 60 hours to write a grant application for $15,000.

The grant from hell was such a waste of time I decided to conduct a cost-benefit analysis. I wanted to examine the cost per hour required to work on the grant application and reports, and the income it produced. I then compared the results to the cost per hour I spent in one-on-one meetings with donors (including preparation and follow up time) and the income per hour those meetings produced. The results were shocking.

Grant from hell:

Hours spent working on the grant application: 60
Hours spent writing four quarterly reports: 120
Hours spent writing year-end report: 30

Total hours working on grant: 210

Income from grant: $15,000

Income per hour of grant writing: **$71**
($15,000 ÷ 210 hours)

One-on-one meetings with major donors:

Hours spent in one-on-one meetings with 40 major donors: 60
Hours spent preparing for meetings and following up: 120

Total hours managing donors: 180

Income from one-on-one meetings: $935,000

Income per hour of one-on-one meetings: **$5,194**
($935,000 ÷ 180 hours)

In this simplified example, the income per hour spent meeting with donors was 73 times ($5,194 ÷ $71) more "profitable" than income per work hour spent on writing the grant. Wow, 73 times! Just think how much money I might have raised had I spent 210 hours in one-hour one-on-one meetings instead of 210 hours working on the grant.

I'll never know the answer, but if I use the figures above for the sake of driving home my point about the efficiency and effectiveness of one-on-one meetings, the potential income could have been an astounding $1,090,740! (210 hours x $5,194 per hour).

Note! Writing grants can be a very effective method of raising money. Some organizations raise millions each year writing grants. Just remember, the average grant lasts only two years! But a donor can give for five years, 10 years, even into perpetuity if they leave you a bequest. Plus, donors can provide time, money, expertise, influence, connections, and be mission ambassadors. That's HUGE value. No grant can do that!

What about galas? Should you have one? Perhaps. To host one may require thousands of hours in labor and cost thousands of dollars. The awareness is good. It collectively inspires donors. It raises money. The question is how much money and benefit will you *net* after subtracting out time and expenses (including staff wages)? In the end, writing grants and hosting galas is resource and return game. Play it wisely!

The lesson to remember, and the one I cannot urge you strongly enough to apply as early in your lifecycle as possible, is this: The most efficient and effective way to raise money is to spend as much time as possible in one-on-one meetings or in small group settings with *major* donors and those controlling funding opportunities at foundations and businesses.

If you're battling limited resources, you need to do whatever it takes to increase the amount of time you spend doing one-on-one fundraising and decrease the time you spend on other fundraising tactics. This means spending more time setting up coffee, lunch, and dinner meetings and less time writing grants, organizing galas, and sending mailers.

Fundraising is a dynamic process. A lot must happen before and after a one-on-one meeting to increase your chances of receiving funding and, more importantly, to create an environment to receive funding year after year. Here are a handful of tactics and tips to get you on the right track, right from the start.

Tactics and Tips

Identify and qualify major donors

The first thing you need to do before meeting major donors is to identify and qualify them. Start by defining what a "major donor" is based on donation size. Keep it simple. Is it a donor who gives $500, $1,000, $5,000, $10,000, or $50,000?

Typically, the larger the budget, the higher the figure used to define a major donor. For example, the budget for a startup nonprofit may be less than $100,000. In this case, a major donor may be defined as a person who gives $1,000 or more. However, a more mature nonprofit may have a budget of $1 million and define a major donor as a person who gives $10,000 or more. If you're not sure what amount to use as a benchmark, use one percent of your budget.

If you're lucky enough to have a donor list, you'll want to comb it and pick out those who qualify as "major." If you don't have a list, you'll need to build one. Start by talking with board members, staff, volunteers, business partners, and anyone who knows, or may have a close connection to, a potential major donor who may have an interest in supporting your mission.

Keep your expectations in check; building a major donor list from scratch is difficult. It requires time and effort (years in some cases) and requires a steadfast, ongoing commitment by the chief executive, board, volunteers, and those on your fundraising team.

If you persevere, the payoff will prove to be one of the best investments of time and energy you ever made. If you have any aspirations of becoming a gold standard nonprofit, you must realize early on that major donors are the golden eggs of funding, and you need to incubate and hatch as many as possible to sustain your nonprofit and fulfill your mission.

Once you have a list of potential major donors, you'll want to use an affordable and easy-to-use contact database program to track donor information, calls, and donations. Don't blow off this process. If you do, you'll be making the same painful mistake many nonprofits make as their number of donors increases, and it will cost unimaginable amounts of time and aggravation to clean up the mess. Be smarter than the rest; buy a contact database program early on and use it.

After entering your donor prospects into your database program, you'll want to evaluate and rank them according to their ability to give, their desire to give, and their relationship with your nonprofit.

You'll also want to find out any personal information you can about the prospects. You don't need much, but showing up to a first-time meeting knowing a tidbit or two about a prospect's interests, hobbies, business, family, or alma mater can go a long way toward breaking the ice and building a relationship.

To find out this type of information, talk with staff, board members, or other people connected with your nonprofit who may know the prospect. Whatever information you discover, enter it into your database, so you can track and update it as the relationship develops.

Find the right match

Once you've identified and qualified prospects, you need to divide them among the *askers* of your nonprofit. Askers are people who are knowledgeable about your nonprofit, have fundraising experience, and are willing to ask for money. This includes the chief executive, board members, fundraising staff, volunteers, members of a fundraising committee, or anyone who has a passion for raising funds to support your mission.

As you now know, establishing strong personal relationships with prospective donors is a key element to raising big money. Personal relationships are rooted in making personal connections, which means you'll want to do the best job you can matching a prospect's interests, hobbies, and background with that of an asker. You'll also want to consider other matching factors such as age, gender, values, beliefs, and income level.

I wish I could say there is a simple formula to match donors with askers, but there isn't. Sometimes younger donors enjoy working with older board members and staff, and sometimes older donors enjoy working with younger people. It's sort of like dating; no matter how much you think two people might be a good fit for each other, you never know until they actually go out.

You don't know for sure which donor is going to match up best with a particular asker, but the more you can increase the likelihood a donor and asker will develop a long-term, close relationship—a friendship—the greater the likelihood you'll receive a series of major gifts.

Get a meeting

Forget mail. Forget email. Forget blogs. If you want to raise money from major donors, you need to set up one-on-one meetings. Major donors give to issues and missions they care about and to people they know and trust. You establish trust by building relationships, and what better way to build a relationship than by spending time together—in person.

It's your responsibility to start the relationship building cycle. Pick up the phone and ask donors to join you for coffee, lunch, a hike, or a meeting at their office.

Often times, a board member or volunteer is the person who has the relationship with a prospect, but is not the person who will be meeting the prospect to make an appeal. In this case, the person with the relationship should attend the first meeting if only to introduce the prospect to the asker and establish a comfortable, friendly setting for the meeting.

This type of introduction is also a convenient way to establish the asker's credibility. "Jim, meet Christy Jacobson, our new chief executive. You'll enjoy talking with her. Like you, she graduated from Yale. She also played soccer on the U.S. National Team for six years. Our staff loves her and she's doing an amazing job launching our two new programs and orchestrating the capital campaign for the new building. I know you'll enjoy talking with her and swapping Yale stories. Have a great meeting."

The purpose of the first meeting, even if it's at cultivation event, is to meet the prospect and establish a relationship. It's not to ask for money, though you should be prepared to discuss the topic if it comes up. Whether it's you or someone else setting up the meeting, the prospect should clearly understand your intention is to get to know them and for them to get to know you, and to learn more about your nonprofit.

Doing this will remove much of the financial "pressure" many donors feel when they meet fundraisers, and it increases the chances of creating a relaxing, lighthearted atmosphere for the meeting, regardless where it takes place.

The day before the meeting, send a reminder email to confirm the time, place, and purpose of the meeting. Keep the email short, only two or three lines. Include pertinent information about the meeting in the subject line of the email, "Reminder: Meeting with Christy Jacobson this Friday–4pm–Spice House Café."

This small gesture will win you a few responsibility points. Major donors are busy. They travel a lot and their schedules change constantly. Things get lost in the shuffle. They forget. I'd say 20 percent of the time after sending out a reminder email, I'd receive a response back from donors thanking me because they had forgotten the appointment or did not have their calendar with them.

Be kind, patient, and persistent
Setting up a meeting with a wealthy prospect can be a time of frustration and rejection. They own businesses, travel, maintain hectic social schedules, and get bombarded by all types of requests, including funding requests from nonprofits. You may ask kindly for a meeting and still not get one.

However, failing to get a meeting does not mean a prospect isn't interested in a meeting, nor does it mean a prospect isn't interested in supporting you; it may just mean the timing isn't right.

For example, you may feel rejected when, for the *fourth* time, an executive assistant of a prospective donor says, "Mr. Jones is out of the office again. This time he's traveling to New York on business. Sorry, you'll have to call back, but I will leave him a message."

Shaking your head, you think to yourself, "I've already left three messages, so why leave a fourth." You say thank you and hang up, and your hopes of getting a meeting vanish.

If a scenario like this happens to you, don't give up and don't say goodbye. Whether it's the first call or the fourth, end the call with a few qualifying questions such as, "When is Mr. Jones returning?" "May I make an appointment with him through you?" "Is one day of the week better than another for scheduling appointments with Mr. Jones?" "Is there a time of day he prefers to have meetings?"

Wealthy and influential people lead busy lives. Many are extremely philanthropic and more eager to help quality nonprofits than you might imagine. Respecting their time and personal space will go a long way toward establishing the relationship and credibility you desire. The goal is to be kind, grateful, patient, and persistent. If you are, you'll get your meeting.

Get to know them

Let's pretend you're the chief executive for a fast-growing nonprofit located in Sun Valley, Idaho. Let's also pretend Dale Kelly is the biggest real estate developer in the county and he's also one of the biggest philanthropists. Last night, your board chair bumped into Dale at a gallery opening and Dale expressed interest in supporting your cause. Great news!

The next morning, you call his office. His assistant answers and works with you to set up a coffee meeting at noon on Monday. You'll have one hour. Before hanging up, you grab her email address and promise to send her an annual report and an "overview" document she can print and share with Dale.

On Monday, you arrive at Dale's office five minutes before noon. You're traveling light, carrying only a folder containing a notepad and some marketing material. Sitting in the waiting room, you remind yourself the purpose of the first meeting is to establish a relationship. You make a commitment to spend the majority of time getting to know Dale and keeping the mood lighthearted.

It's important for Dale to see and feel your passion for your mission, so you'll want to make sure you share the latest news about the good work your nonprofit is doing with genuine enthusiasm.

Dale also wants to believe your nonprofit is effective and worthy of support. To do this, you need to be prepared to answer any question he might throw your way. "Why did the founder quit?" "Why are you downsizing your newest program?" "Tell me how you plan to pay off your mortgage?" "If I give you $10,000, what will you do with it?" "How much of your funding goes toward programming?" "What's your vision for the next three years?"

If Dale is like most major donors, he likes to buy things from people he likes and trusts, so if you're the asker, you'll want to make sure you spend a little time talking about yourself. Be humble and sincere, but be confident about sharing your successes and background. Donors are especially interested in knowing how you got involved with your nonprofit and why you're passionate about the cause. You should be prepared to express all this in a smooth and compelling five-minute story.

Once the meeting is underway, it's your job to control the tempo, tone, and topics of the conversation. Conversation should be genuine, personal, and two-way. Ask open-ended questions and encourage donors to talk. "Dale, how did you meet John, our board chair?" "Why did you and Megan decide to move here from your home in Hawaii?" "What did you enjoy most about working at the embassy in Switzerland?"

My favorite questions center on interests and hobbies because everyone likes talking about things they enjoy doing. "Dale, I heard you fly airplanes; how did that come about?" "John told me you play bass guitar and once jammed with the legendary Buddy Guy; tell me the story."

It's good to be inquisitive during a meeting, but you need to remain sensitive and subtle. You want to avoid making someone like Dale feel like he is taking part in a probing interview hosted by Anderson Cooper.

Eventually, you'll want to find out why a donor like Dale has an interest in your organization. Keep the question simple. For example, if I knew Dale had an interest in supporting our children's day camp, I'd ask, "Tell me, why are you drawn to help children with disabilities?"

As the conversation unfolds, I would be constantly on the lookout for ways Dale's interests, values, and beliefs overlap with the mission, culture, and programming of SVAS, and the interests, values, and beliefs of our staff, board, and volunteers.

This is important because the interests, values, and beliefs Dale holds are probably at the core of what has motivated him to take an interest in our work. The more alignment I discover, the greater my chances of linking Dale to SVAS on a deeper, emotional level.

If an opportunity presents itself, toss in some humor. You'll find laughter goes a long way toward building personal relationships and raising money. When donors ask where I grew up, I don't say Wisconsin, I say "I'm a Cheesehead!" It always gets a chuckle.

Keep the first meeting to an hour or less. About 15 minutes before the end of the meeting, ask "Are we okay on time?" Read their body language. End the meeting if you sense they want—or need—to go.

Keeping the meeting under the allotted time will earn you a slice of respect.

End the meeting by graciously thanking the donor for his time and tell him how you'll follow up. "Dale, I'll send the financial information you requested and follow up with a call late next week—how's that sound?"

The second meeting: Show 'em the goods

A week later, you call Dale to set up a second meeting. His assistant patches you through and Dale pops on the phone with a friendly tone and says, "Hi, Tom! Glad you called. Megan and I read your material and watched the video you suggested. The work you guys are doing is outstanding. We're very impressed and we would like to learn more."

With a response like that, you know Dale and Megan are on board. Your goal now is to set up a second meeting. The purpose of the second meeting is to deepen your relationship, answer detailed questions about your nonprofit, and make an appeal. The meeting could be at his office, your office, his home, or a nice place for lunch or a glass of wine. If you go out, choose a place that's comfortable and classy, but not extravagant. And you would definitely want to invite Megan to the meeting.

When talking with Dale, be prepared to suggest a time and place for the meeting, but if your suggestion doesn't work, be quick to follow up and say, "What time and place would work best for you and Megan?"

One of my favorite tactics for making first time appeals with major donors at SVAS was scheduling lunch meetings in close proximity to where one of our programs was taking place. For example, there is a restaurant located at the Sun Valley Resort called Gretchen's. It has patio seating facing a historic, outdoor, open-air ice rink where our children with disabilities took ice skating lessons in July. If prospective donors like Dale and Megan were interested in supporting our summer day camp program, a lunch at Gretchen's is where I'd take them.

The restaurant serves delicious food in a casual setting with majestic mountain views as a backdrop. Even better, the outdoor patio sits adjacent to the ice rink, so donors like Dale and Megan could watch our children with Down syndrome, Asperger's, and autism learn to ice skate while they ate lunch and asked questions about the program and SVAS.

After lunch, I'd take prospective donors for a walk around the rink. This way, they'd get a close-up view of the program and see how our instructors taught children with disabilities how to ice skate. I'd introduce them to a few staff and then get them out on the ice to hold the hand of a child and skate around. This always proved to be a powerful, heart-warming moment. I also knew that once a couple like Dale and Megan "touched" the program, and saw the life-changing impact we were making on children with disabilities, they would instantly become emotionally connected to the program and our mission.

Once you emotionally connect a donor, asking for money almost takes care of itself. Lunch meetings at Gretchen's and the ice rink usually ended with prospective donors saying something like, "Your organization is doing amazing work and we'd love to support it; tell us how we can help?" When you hear a comment like this, it's time to make an appeal.

For a second meeting, you may prefer to meet a donor for lunch, dinner, or a glass of wine. These are all very effective settings to raise money, and I'm sure you can think of many more. I've raised money in airplanes and taxicabs, and on tennis courts and ski slopes. Where you meet donors for a second meeting is important, but it's not as important as deepening your personal relationship with them and emotionally connecting them to your work and mission.

Let donors see and feel your passion
Passion is powerful. Whether it's your first meeting with a donor or your tenth, one of the most powerful ways to emotionally connect a donor to your mission and raise money is to let them see and feel *your* passion. It doesn't matter if you're the chief executive, board secretary, or fundraising team member, if you're asking donors for money, they expect to see the sparkle in your eyes and feel the passion in your soul when you talk about your nonprofit.

This is why people with introverted personalities should not be your primary fundraisers. Also, never force people to ask for money. Negative or fearful people can turn off donors and you may lose them forever. Money is the lifeblood of your nonprofit, and you need the right people on your fundraising team who can deliver the goods in a big way.

If you're a small nonprofit, it's unlikely you have the funds to hire a professional fundraiser with 10 years of experience. That's okay. With a small budget, you can still have tremendous fundraising success by hiring or training exceptionally talented people with less experience.

I've had great success hiring recent college graduates. I look for individuals who are smart, motivated, enthusiastic, and have a track record of taking initiative and achieving success. They must have at least some experience in sales, marketing, or fundraising, and demonstrate the ability to influence. I ask myself, "Would this person inspire me to write a $10,000 check and join his cause?" If the answer is yes, they may just land themselves a job as a fundraiser.

I learned long ago that the amount of money spent on salaries of fundraising staff is not correlated to how much money they can raise. Remember, people like to give to people they like and trust. If you have a limited budget and want to increase your chances of raising big money from major donors, build a fundraising staff made up of likeable and reliable people with exceptional communication skills.

What if you have no budget to hire fundraising staff? If you're in this position, like most small nonprofits, you'll need to build a fundraising team by enlisting your most dynamic and confident staff, board members, and volunteers.

At the top of this list should be your chief executive. She *must* be a remarkable fundraiser. No one is in a better position to meet donors, share important information about your nonprofit, and tell compelling stories.

Boards know this, and many boards place too much fundraising responsibility on the chief executive. As I mentioned, the SVAS board placed nearly all the fundraising responsibility on my shoulders. Most members wanted little to do with fundraising and they weren't about to change.

Boards that have policies like this do an injustice to their chief executive, the nonprofit, and the nonprofit industry. Fundraising is typically a full-time job in itself. How can a board reasonably expect a chief executive to manage all facets of operations, programming, and staff management, and do all the fundraising? Something will give—and it's usually the will of the executive, resulting in frustration and burnout.

No matter what the size of your nonprofit, the *maximum* amount of time your chief executive should spend raising money is 50 percent. I suggest a target of 35-40 percent. This includes all the time necessary to manage fundraising support functions such as phone calls, follow-up letters, and developing collateral material.

If you keep your chief executive's fundraising obligations to 35-40 percent and allocate the other 60-65 percent to board members (see pages 97-99), volunteers, or fundraising staff, you should be able to raise all the money you need to sustain your nonprofit.

If your chief executive is not a good fundraiser, and you have trouble rallying board members and volunteers to help raise money, you'll struggle raising money until you can develop, or hire, a team of experienced fundraisers.

Whether your team of fundraisers is experienced or inexperienced, the success of their fundraising efforts will depend greatly on their passion for the mission and their passion for raising money to support it.

If you raise funds for your nonprofit and you want to emotionally connect donors to your mission, let them see, feel, and hear *your* passion. Let donors see your excitement through your warm smile and positive body language. Let them feel your enthusiasm when you tell them what motivates you to raise money to fulfill the mission, and let them hear your passion through the upbeat tone in your voice.

Donors expect to see and feel your passion. If it's genuine and contagious, donors will notice, and you'll raise more money more quickly than you ever imagined.

Just ask
Studies show 80 percent of the people who made their last contribution did so simply because someone asked. You're ready! Let's say you've established personal relationships with major donors like Dale and Megan. They've seen your program in action, met the staff, visited your offices, reviewed case for support material, watched a video, scoured financial statements, asked tough questions, and listened to convincing reasons why your noble programming is worthy of support.

Dale and Megan like you and believe in you and your mission. They say they want to help; so it's now time to ask for a contribution.

Believe it or not, the majority of major donors enjoy giving money away. They feel honored when asked for a contribution, even if they must decline. Of course, you must choose an appropriate moment to ask and do so in a gracious and modest manner, but the most important thing you must do when raising money, and often the most challenging thing to do, is actually ask for it.

Wait for the right moment
When I think the time is right to make an appeal, I wait for a relaxed moment in a conversation when I sense a donor's body language is positive, the energy between us is friendly, and our conversation is upbeat. When the moment arrives, I make a simple and straightforward appeal:

> "Dale and Megan, would you be willing to make a $5,000 donation to sponsor five children to attend our summer day camp?"

Or,

> "Dale and Megan, I want to thank you for your $8,000 contribution last year. As you recall, it allowed us to buy two adaptive bi-skis. This year, we would like to add two mono-skis to our fleet. They cost $5,000 each. Would you be willing to fund the purchase of these mono-skis with a contribution of $10,000?"

Be reasonable
Keep the appeal reasonable. It would be unreasonable, and possibly offensive, to ask a prospective donor who earns $500,000 a year for a $100,000 contribution. Even if a prospect has the ability to make a substantial contribution, it's best to keep a first-time appeal modest. In this case, an appeal of $2,500 or $5,000 would be more appropriate. As you build trust, establish a relationship, and prove your value, you can ask for larger contributions.

Create matching gift opportunities
Major donors like to make contributions when they know other major donors, especially friends, are making contributions. When possible, use a gift table and try to create matching gift opportunities, sponsorship opportunities, or a "wish list" of items you need and donors can "buy":

"Dale and Megan, we're in the process of raising $70,000 for a 21-passenger, wheelchair accessible bus for our children's summer day camp. We're offering $10,000 sponsorships and we've already secured six other commitments. In fact, your good friends, Bob and Fran Smith, bought two. We need only one more. Would you be willing to fund the final sponsorship slot?"

Handle objections with confidence

After you ask, just listen. Say nothing until they do. Not a word. If they say "yes," great! If they decline your appeal, or balk in some way, there's probably a good reason. Perhaps they have looming tuition bills for their kids. Maybe they recently lost a lot of money in the stock market. Perhaps they planned to make a large contribution to their alma mater. Maybe they would rather hear the appeal from a friend who sits on your board. Or, maybe they would rather make an in-kind gift.

Whatever the reason, and there are dozens, a donor's decision not to donate is not necessarily a rejection of you, your nonprofit, or their interest in making a contribution. This is a reality all successful fundraisers understand and accept.

When donors object, and they will, there is no need to sulk and feel like a failure. Rather, seize the opportunity and discover their reasons for objecting. Once you find out, you can work on strategies to address their concerns and find solutions to their objections.

Here's a simple, surefire 3-step process that you can use when handling objections:

1. **Acknowledge.** Acknowledge the objection with empathy.
2. **Solution.** Find a solution by providing options.
3. **Close.** Close and thank. Or, agree to next steps.

Examples:

"Dale and Megan, after hearing about your father's illness, I understand the timing is bad right now. Our annual fundraiser isn't for another six months; how about I call you a month or so before the event?"

Or,

"Dale and Megan, I sense you want to make a gift, but it sounds like my appeal of $10,000 is too high. Would a $5,000 gift be more in line with the amount you were hoping to give?"

Or,

"Dale and Megan, I can understand how you might *feel* that $5,000 is too much money right now. I was asked recently for $2,500 and *felt* the same way. However, when they offered to break up the $2,500 into four quarterly payments, I *found* that I could make the gift. Would a $5,000 gift work for you if we broke it up into four quarterly payments of $1,250?"

Take pride in asking for money

When asking for money, you should feel proud and honored, not embarrassed or ashamed. It should be a time of celebration and a chance to express your passion and share the good news about the great work you're doing. If your nonprofit is truly doing amazing work and you're running a gold standard operation with a team of star performers, you'll find plenty of joyful givers.

Let me leave you with one last story. During the summer of my senior year in high school, I sold Kirby vacuum cleaners. My boss was a bald southerner who had been in sales all his life. Five days a week, five hours a day, he had us canvass neighborhoods selling $600 vacuum cleaners to people who couldn't afford them. I still feel guilty thinking about it.

Most of that job remains a blur, but I'll always remember my boss roaming around the office from desk to desk with a cup of coffee in one hand and a chocolate donut in the other shouting, "You can't get the sale unless you ask! You can't get the sale unless you ask!"

I've never forgotten this barked maxim. It's helped me raise millions of dollars over the years and it can help you raise millions too. You've worked hard to begin building a great organization. Take initiative, pride, and pleasure in asking people to support it. I guarantee you'll be happy with the responses.

The tactics above are only a handful of the most important fundraising strategies you can use to raise money. There are scores of workshops and resources available to help you improve the effectiveness of your fundraising efforts. Tap into these resources so you can maintain a competitive advantage over nonprofits too naive to do the same. If you're interested in a practical, how-to fundraising book for your board and staff, let me suggest my latest book, *Cloudburst*. You can check out reviews and buy the most recent version at a discount at TomIselin.com.

Takeaways

You're busy and resources are scarce. You can't afford to spend six months and 2,500 hours to organize a gala that nets only $60,000. You don't have time to spend 60 hours writing a grant application that may or may not bring you $15,000, and you can't afford to send out a fundraising mailer that takes 50 hours to design and costs $4,000 to produce and mail, yet raises only $8,000.

With time and money at a premium, you need to maximize the amount of time and money you spend raising money. The most time-efficient and cost-effective way to do this is to hold personal, one-on-one meetings with major donors.

Instead of spending 60 hours writing a grant, imagine if you met with 60 major donors for 60 one-hour meetings. If you raised an *average* of $2,000 from each meeting, you'd raise $120,000! Some donors may give more, some less, and some not at all, but you get the point—it's a lot of money. If your budget is $260,000, it's *a lot* of money!

Managing a pool of major donors is not only the most efficient and effective way to raise money, it's also a reliable fundraising tactic to sustain a nonprofit. Think about it. Would you rather rely on a few grants and a fundraiser to sustain your nonprofit, or 30 major donors, each of whom have a passion for your mission and a net worth in the millions?

I'll admit, quality long-term grants and well-organized gala events can raise big money, and you should absolutely incorporate them into your fundraising mix. But they can also be risky undertakings. What will you do when the grant cycle stops? What will you do when the pool of grantors dwindles? What if the gala auctioneer doesn't do a good job? What if the turnout is small? What happens if the celebrity comedian you invited cancels at the last minute? What happens if you raise only half the money you hoped to raise? I'll tell you what happens—you'll freak out!

If you want to ensure short-term and long-term financial security, and worry a lot less, build the biggest network of donors—large and small—that you can. Invest time and effort to develop deep, personal relationships with as many donors as possible and find ways to emotionally connect them to your mission. Then provide "concierge stewardship" which means going above and beyond to make the donor's experience (with everything) unexpectedly pleasurable. If successful, you'll not only lay the cornerstone of financial sustainability for your nonprofit, you'll find yourself the recipient of many unexpected blessings and benefits.

For one, you can expect some of your donors will become powerful ambassadors, sharing the great work you're doing with wealthy friends, business partners, and media executives. Others will become star volunteers and strategic partners, helping you solve problems and achieve goals by using their expertise and influence. You've heard it a hundred times, "It's all about relationships." Make it happen.

If you want to be a gold standard nonprofit and achieve fundraising success that far exceeds your expectations, make this statement your number one fundraising objective: "Fifty percent of our fundraising effort will be spent making appeals to major donors in personal, one-on-one settings." Over the long run, no fundraising tactic has the potential to raise more money in a shorter period of time with the least amount of effort and create the greatest likelihood of financial sustainability. Not one.

And last . . . just ask! More donors than you think want to support your noble work. Engage them in your mission, emotionally connect them to your programming, make a good case for support, and express *your* passion for your mission.

When the moment is right, ask for a donation, because you won't get one unless you ask! If you ask humbly and graciously, the answer more often than not will be a delightful and generous "Yes!"

Want to raise more money?
Visit TomIselin.com. You'll find how-to tutorials and strategies to help you become a star fundraiser and build a winning fundraising program.

CHAPTER 15

Wisdom Network
Surrounding yourself with knowledge and experience

The nonprofit world is a quirky one. Many nonprofits are founded by passionate people with little or no nonprofit experience. Many board members have little or no nonprofit experience, and many staff members have little or no nonprofit and business experience.

The result is often a lot of wasted time and effort. Mistakes are made, resources are poorly allocated, and problems are ignored. People get involved and things get done, but no one is sure what *should* be done, how it should be done, or who should be responsible to do what.

A nonprofit can avoid many of these common pitfalls by establishing a "wisdom network." A wisdom network is nothing more than a network of people, organizations, and resources that can help a nonprofit run more efficiently and effectively by providing information, knowledge, skills, and experience.

This is a bonus chapter. It's only two pages, but its contents are fundamental to any nonprofit trying to build a gold standard nonprofit.

Build a network with people
Many seasoned staff and board members have gone through the same challenges you're facing. Whether it's learning how to file an IRS 990, or learning how to set up a planned giving option for a major donor, others have scratched their heads wondering what to do. You're not the first.

Find out where nonprofit executives and board members gather in your community. There is usually some type of association or regular meeting sponsored by a community foundation, local nonprofit, or college. Attend these gatherings, meet people, and learn from others.

Establish relationships with experienced board members, chief executives, and key staff. Set up meetings, ask questions, and learn from their mistakes and successes. If you find a good personality fit, ask them to mentor you. Most will say yes, and be honored you asked.

Build of network of organizations

You can learn a lot from people, but you can also learn from organizations. Some may be in your community, some may be in your industry, and some may have a similar nonprofit structure. Reach out to best practice organizations you feel you can benefit from knowing.

The latest buzz in the nonprofit world is "collaboration" and "collective impact." You'll want to look for ways to collaborate with organizations in your community or your industry to share resources and ideas to achieve common goals and purposes.

However, be warned. Collaboration sounds good in theory, but it can burn up time and resources. My advice is to embrace collaboration thoughtfully. Examine the benefits, costs, and outcomes, and then prudently allocate resources to manage your collaborative efforts.

Build a network of resources

Running a gold standard nonprofit is complicated. For this reason alone, your staff, board, and volunteers should always be exploring ways to refine their skills and learn how to run a best practice nonprofit.

You'll find more than a dozen useful resources in the Resources section of this book. You'll also want to read books and magazines, subscribe to websites and blogs, join associations and trade groups, and attend conferences and workshops. These are all excellent resources for learning how to improve skills and run a high-performance nonprofit. Make sure you budget funds to pay for these types of resources.

Takeaways

Building a wisdom network is one of the most undervalued and underused techniques a nonprofit can use to build a gold standard nonprofit. The nonprofit world may be quirky, but it is also gracious. People and organizations are typically very willing to share what they've learned to help other nonprofits climb the rungs of success. All you need to do is show up, meet people, and humbly ask for help.

Parting Words

Thank you for reading this book. I hope you learned many useful principles, tactics, tips, tools, and insights. If you apply what you've learned, people will notice. Donors and foundations will notice. Industry peers will notice. Media will notice. Volunteers will notice. Your entire community will notice. The result will be a high-performance nonprofit that everyone is proud to support.

I'm sure you have big dreams for your noble mission. Awesome! To give yourself the greatest chance of success and to separate yourself from competing nonprofits, you must make wise choices early on and throughout the life of your nonprofit.

I wrote *First Things First* because I want to help people like you dodge the costly blunders most nonprofits make. I certainly made my share. I did things in the wrong order, took short cuts, hired unskilled staff, selected disengaged board members, and waited too long to make a change when change was in order.

One of the most painful lessons every seasoned nonprofit leader learns is that seemingly harmless blunders made early on often have long-term—very long-term—consequences that can stall or derail the hopes and dreams of a great mission.

You'll make your share of blunders, that's a given. However, I hope you'll use *First Things First* as a guidebook to help you build a gold standard nonprofit and minimize the size and number of blunders you make along the way.

Let me also say, it's easy to set standards of performance and integrity, but it's very difficult to sustain a system of accountability that holds a nonprofit, and the people connected with it, accountable to such standards. Nonetheless, you have a moral, ethical, and social responsibility to do just that.

Remember, it's not what you do, it's *how* you do what you do that separates you from the pack. And just because you can do something, *should* you do it? Ask yourself "why?" more often.

Starting a nonprofit is relatively easy. However, building and sustaining a gold standard nonprofit is one of the most challenging tasks you'll ever undertake. It's also one of the most rewarding. If you address the truths of what you must do to become a gold standard nonprofit and have the passion, perseverance, and integrity to fulfill these truths, your nonprofit will be a triumphant success.

It all starts with doing the right things, right from the start.

First Things First!

Resources

The Internet is a great place for finding additional resources to help you build a gold standard nonprofit. Instead of providing resources for each topic covered in the book, I'm providing a handful of portal sites that will lead you to hundreds of useful resources.

American Branding Association (branding)
www.americanbranding.org

American Management Association (management)
www.amanet.org

American Marketing Association (marketing)
www.marketingpower.com

Ashoka (social entrepreneurialism)
www.ashoka.org

Association of Fundraising Professionals (fundraising)
www.afpnet.org

BoardSource (boards and executives)
www.boardsource.org

Chronicle of Philanthropy (philanthropy/general nonprofit)
www.philanthropy.com

DoSomething (youth volunteering)
www.dosomething.org

Foundation Center (philanthropy/general nonprofit)
www.foundationcenter.org

GuideStar (nonprofit reporting)
www.guidestar.org

Internal Revenue Service (general nonprofit)
www.irs.gov/charities

Management Library (general nonprofit/management)
www.managementhelp.org

National Speakers Association (public speaking)
www.nsaspeaker.org

Nonprofit Times (general nonprofit)
www.nptimes.com

Points of Light (volunteering)
www.pointsoflight.org

SparkWise (data collection to demonstrate impact)
www.sparkwise.com

Society for Human Resources Management (human resources)
www.shrm.org

Society for Nonprofit Organizations (general nonprofit)
www.snpo.org

Stanford Social Innovation Review (social entrepreneurialism)
www.ssireview.org

Tech Soup (technology)
www.techsoup.org

Toastmasters International (public speaking)
www.toastmasters.org

Writer's Digest (writing)
www.writersdigest.com

Index

First Things First
Business Services

• Practical Solutions   • Wise Advice   • Happy Clients

Need help? With more than 20 years of experience working with nonprofit and for-profit organizations, I've seen just about every situation, challenge, and drama imaginable.

Whether you're a startup food pantry, a fast-growing art center trying to bolster fundraising, or an established homeless shelter looking to build capacity, I offer a variety of services that can help your team overcome its challenges and embrace effective and innovative solutions to build a gold standard nonprofit that propels your noble mission.

All retreats and workshops are *customized* to fit the needs of your board retreat, staff workshop, strategic planning session, or conference.

Retreats, Workshops and Services
(Fees are scaled: based on budget size and number of staff)
- Board and staff retreats
- Strategic planning and visioning
- Capacity building; organizational development
- Culture development for board, staff, and organization
- Governance training; board development
- High impact fundraising plans
- Face-to-face solicitation tactics; major gift tactics
- Fundraising audits; gala effectiveness assessments
- And many others . . . call me!

Also, visit my website. You'll find video tutorials, podcasts, information, and resources that will help you sharpen your skills and keep you connected with others who are passionate about running thriving nonprofits that donors are thrilled to support.

TomIselin.com
tomiselin@gmail.com   858.888.2278